# ON THE MUSIC OF THE NORTH AMERICAN INDIANS

Theodore Baker's monograph (Leipzig 1882):
original German text and English translation by
Ann Buckley

# ON THE MUSIC OF THE NORTH AMERICAN INDIANS

BY

THEODORE BAKER

TRANSLATED BY ANN BUCKLEY

DA CAPO PRESS · NEW YORK · 1977

ISBN 0-306-70888-4

199009

# CONTENTS

# FOREWORD TO THE TRANSLATION

Theodore Baker's doctoral thesis at the University of Leipzig, *Über die Musik der nordamerikanischen Wilden*[1], has been called 'the first serious study' of north American Indian Music (*Harvard Dictionary of Music*, ed. W. Apel, Cambridge, Mass. 1973, s.v., 'American Indian Music'), and 'the first strictly musicological monograph published by an American' (Gilbert Chase in *Perspectives in Musicology*, New York 1972, p. 208). The need for an English translation was also referred to by Chase, who observed: 'Deplorably, this has never been reprinted or published in an English translation' (ibid., n. 16). The object of the present publication is to make available within one cover Baker's text and a translation into English.

Baker's thought-patterns, in terms both of musical analysis and of anthropological viewpoints, deserve study in their own right within the framework of the history of ideas. It has been the aim of the translator to transmit intact Baker's ways of thinking, as far as this is possible, without attempting to update either his presuppositions or his vocabulary. Not that his topics are outdated − by no means. His discussion of the 'immanence' of music-language, and his observations on the musicality of people who from earliest childhood watch and join in the dances of their society are among those still relevant to current work. In the main, two kinds of problem arise − that of penetrating and transferring to another language the author's lines of argument, and that of maintaining both logic and consistency in the translation of technical terminology. On the former point, differences of opinion may well arise. On the latter, some specific decisions were made, which may call for some explanation. Baker's term *Tonart*, where it is clearly applied to a discussion of tune, is translated 'tonality', used in the sense of tune-tonality (see, e.g., Paul Hindemith, *The Craft of Musical Composition*, vol. II, New York 1941, p. [3]: 'A melody consists of tone-steps and tone-skips, in so far as the purely *melodic* activity of the interval progression is concerned, apart from its rhythmic and *harmonic* contents' (italics by F.H.). In the discussion of classical Greek modes, however, *Tonart* is translated 'mode'. Baker's term *Grundton*, also in a tune context, is translated as '(tonal) centre' or as 'tonic' (from p. 13 on, with reference to a stated note). *Tonleiter* is rendered as 'scale' (but on p. 15 as 'gamut'), and *Tonsystem* as 'note-system'.

For purposes of convenience, an order of the material has been adopted in which: (1) the English translation (with the footnotes grouped at the end) follows immediately after Baker's text; (2) his Notated Examples come next, and are interleaved with the translation of their accompanying text; and (3) there follow Baker's Tables and Plates, and a list of writings cited by him. Baker's incomplete and inconsistently presented bibliographical information has been removed from the footnote translations, and the information in the List of Works has been regularised according to current practice, and in some instances supplemented in terms of more recent editions and/or citations of

---

1. Leipzig 1882, with the first name spelt Theodor.

editions in the original language. Translator's footnotes are indicated by letters, and are shown at the foot of the page. Baker's list of *errata* has been incorporated in the translation, and in a few cases inaccuracies in his material have been corrected. For easier cross-reference, Baker's page-numbers are shown in the left-hand margin of the translation.

Frank Harrison

Amsterdam
28 March 1976

*Medicin Pipe-Stem Dance* by Paul Kane

Courtesy Royal Ontario Museum, Toronto/Canada

# ÜBER DIE MUSIK

## DER

# NORDAMERIKANISCHEN WILDEN

VON

## THEODOR BAKER.

LEIPZIG,

DRUCK UND VERLAG VON BREITKOPF & HÄRTEL.

1882.

# VORBEMERKUNG.

Während eines mehrwöchentlichen Aufenthalts in Amerika im Sommer 1880 bot sich dem Verfasser die Gelegenheit, die Senecas, eine im westlichen New York wohnende, dem Stamm der Irokesen angehörige Indianernation, zu besuchen, und durch diesen Besuch den eigentlichen Zweck seiner Reise zu erreichen. Hier hat er nicht nur den verschiedenen Festlichkeiten, welche alljährlich zur Zeit des Erntefests unter den Indianern veranstaltet werden, beigewohnt, sondern hat auch einen der geübtesten Sänger bewogen, ihm nach dem Feste fünfzig bis sechszig Lieder vorzusingen, wovon mehrere (in den Notenbeilagen I bis incl. X) als besonders characteristisch gewählt und aufs sorgfältigste notirt wurden. Vom Commandanten der Training-School for Indian Youth zu Carlisle, Penn[a], eingeladen, begab sich der Verf. dorthin und wurde durch das freundliche Entgegenkommen der dortigen Beamten in den Stand gesetzt, noch zweiundzwanzig Lieder verschiedener Indianernationen seiner Sammlung beizufügen. Diese zweiunddreissig Lieder (I bis incl. XXXII) bilden, in § 3 bis incl. § 6, den eigentlichen Kern der vorliegenden Abhandlung; die übrigen Paragraphen dienen hauptsächlich dazu, die Bedeutung

3

der Musik für den Indianer zu zeigen, und sind keineswegs als erschöpfend zu betrachten; die Indianerpoesie allein wäre ein würdiger Gegenstand für ein umfassendes Werk; eine Beschreibung der unzähligen Tänze und Ceremonien jeder Art, in welchen Musik gebraucht wird, würde viel zu weit führen; der Verf. hat sich also damit begnügt, auf die verschiedenen Quellen aufmerksam zu machen, in welchen er eine Berechtigung für den allgemeinen Character mehrerer Bemerkungen zu finden glaubt. — Ich ergreife diese Gelegenheit folgenden Damen und Herren, welche mir bei den Vorarbeiten mit Rath und That beigestanden, meinen wärmsten Dank auszusprechen: meiner verehrten Mutter Mrs. Elizabeth Hunt, Mrs. H. S. Caswell, Miss H. L. Garratt, Rev. Isaac Baird, Mr. Y. Bonillas, Prof. T. W. Chittenden, Rev. J. Owen Dorsey, Rev. M. Eells, Dr. Wills de Hass, Rev. Horace Edwin Hayden, Maj. J. W. Powell, Capt. R. H. Pratt, Rev. A. L. Riggs, Rev. T. L. Riggs, Rev. John Robinson, Gen. David H. Strother, R. P. Eugène Vetromile, Rev. J. P. Williamson.

LEIPZIG, im März 1881.

**Der Verfasser.**

# INHALT.

# Berichtigungen.

S. 4 Z. 21: M a n g e l s anstatt Mangel.

S. 11 Z. 12 und 15: S h i c é l a k a anstatt Shicé laká.

S. 11 Z. 27: k a - r í - r i anstatt ka.rí-ri.

S. 18 Z. 28: Y. B o n i l l a s anstatt J. Bonillas.

S. 24 Z. 9: L o k r i s c h e n anstatt Hypodorischen.

S. 27 Z. 7: i n D u r n o c h i n M o l l anstatt in Moll.

S. 41 Z. 1: ♩ ♪ anstatt ♩ ♪

S. 45 Z. 15: F o l g e n d e s anstatt folgendes.

S. 49 Z. 23—26 lese man: Fig. 1 ist der einleitende Gesang und zeigt die Abbildung einer für den nächtlichen Tanz eingerichteten Indianerhütte, die mit sieben Kreuzen, welche sieben Leichen vorstellen, geschmückt und mit einem magischen Knochen und mit Federn gekrönt ist.

S. 64 letzte Z.: p é anstatt pi.

S. 66 Z. 5 von unten: w a n - y a n - k i anstatt wan-ya-ka.

S. 74 Z. 1: 🎼 anstatt 🎼

## §. 1. Einleitung.

Durch die Musik, sowohl unter den Wilden wie unter Culturmenschen, gewinnen die Gefühlsäusserungen eine Intensität, welche ihnen durch Worte und Geberden allein nicht verliehen werden kann. Da aber der Wilde, anstatt der Mannigfaltigkeit der Empfindungen, welche in der civilisirten Welt rege sind, verhältnissmässig wenige geistige und sinnliche Triebe fühlt, so bleibt seine Sprache, und mit dieser seine Musik, die Sprache des Gefühls, eine einfache und beschränkte. Wie die beigegebenen Lieder entstanden, wie sie ihre jetzige Gestalt und gewisse Abrundung erhielten, wäre kaum mit Bestimmtheit zu sagen. Der Indianer vereinfacht (für seine Denkungsart) die Antwort auf diese Frage dadurch, dass er solchen Gesängen, die in besonderen religiösen Festen gebraucht werden, einen übernatürlichen Ursprung zuschreibt, [1]) und meint, die neueren Lieder seien nach diesen Mustern gefertigt worden.

---

1) Der seneca Sänger A-ō-doñ-wĕ sagte dem Verf.: »Wir haben die Lieder [zum Erntefest] vom Ha-we-ni-yu« (d. h. Grossen Manne da oben). — Die Mexikaner hatten eine ähnliche Fabel (Clavigero, Geschichte v. Mexiko, Leipzig 1789, Buch 6, Abschn. 3). — In Hayti führte »ein Priester oder Gesetzgeber, Bohito III«, die Musik und Instrumente ein. (Rafinesque, The Amer. Nations, Phila, 1836, vol. I, ch. VI, p. 191). — In Yucatan, und unter den Dakotas, kamen die Instrumente angeblich von den Göttern. — Ueber die Entstehung und Entwickelung der Künste unter den Wilden vergl. »Dr. Brown's Betrachtungen über die Poesie und Musik«, deutsche Uebersetzung von Eschenburg, Leipzig, 1769, Abschn. III und IV. — Nach den kärglichen, sich häufig widersprechenden Nachrichten, welche wir über den Zustand der Musik unter den Mexikanern zur Zeit der spanischen Eroberung erhalten haben,

1

Einige Schriftsteller sind der Meinung, die Indianergesänge seien anfänglich eine blosse Nachahmung gewisser
Vögel gewesen; jedoch zeigen sie keinen geistigen Zusammenhang zwischen solchen trivialen Versuchen und dem wah-
ren und höheren Ausdruck des Gefühls, welcher jede Musik
sein sollte, uud welcher die Musik der Indianer in Wirklich-
keit ist. [1] Viel näher liegt und berechtigter erscheint die
Annahme, dass diese Melodien die Frucht einer langsamen
Evolution sind, welche in den einfachsten, allen Menschen
gemeinsamen Aeusserungen der Freude oder des Schmerzes
wurzelt. [Vergl. »Poesie« und »Rhythmus«]. Diese Annahme
liegt näher, weil ihr zufolge die Musik unmittelbar aus dem
menschlichen Herzen entspringt; berechtigt wird sie durch
den thatsächlichen Zustand der Musik unter den auf den
untersten Stufen der Entwickelung stehenden Indianerstäm-
men; unter solchen aber erscheint der Gesang selten als eine
selbstständige Kunst, sondern fast immer von verschieden-
artigen Tänzen begleitet. — In den Hauptzügen zeigen die
Aufführungen der verschiedenen Indianervölker grosse Aehn-

---

ist es nicht unwahrscheinlich, dass die vom Dr. B. geschilderten »Folgen der Verbesserung der Sitten unter den Wilden«, bis incl. § 31,
mit dem Fortschritt der Musik und verwandten Künsten unter den
aztekischen Völkern die grösste Aehnlichkeit haben. Eine wissenschaft-
liche Untersuchung über diese sehr interessante Frage bedarf der ge-
nauesten, an Ort und Stelle unternommenen Forschungen; der Verf.
der vorliegenden Schrift hat sich daher nur erlaubt, einige zerstreute,
vergleichende Bemerkungen hierüber zu machen. Brasseur de Bourbourg und Torquemada haben bis jetzt auf diesem Gebiete das Meiste
geleistet.

1) Das Nachahmen der Thiere (besonders ihrer körperlichen Bewegungen) erscheint zwar sehr häufig mit den Gesängen verbunden,
nicht aber als integrirender Theil derselben, sondern zur Ergänzung
der dürftigen Worte; die Musik zeigt sich stets als der Ausdruck des
menschlichen Gefühls, welches ganz etwas anderes ist, als eine
Nachahmung der äusseren Natur. Wörter, die den verschiedensten
Naturlauten nachgeahmt worden, kommen wohl in allen Sprachen vor;
aber für die Freude (das Lachen), die Trauer und den Schmerz, hat
der Mensch ganz eigene, seinen Organen und seiner geistigen Natur
passende Ausdrucksarten.

lichkeit unter einander. Franklin [1]) giebt uns folgende Schilderung eines Tanzes der Dogrib-Indianer (Brit. Nord-Amer.) : »Sie stellten sich in einen Kreis und fingen nun mit weit gespreizten Beinen und den Händen auf den Hüften, gleichzeitige, nach seitwärts gerichtete Sprünge zu machen an, bei jedem Sprung die Silbe »tsa« stark herausstossend.«

Hier bewegen sich die Tanzenden im Kreise, wie es wohl unter allen Indianernationen bei gewissen Festen gebräuchlich ist; [2]) dazu gleichzeitig, streng rhythmisch, ein höchst charakteristischer, in fast allen musikalischen Aufführungen zu bemerkender Zug, [3]) wie ebenfalls das Zusammensingen; die monotone Wiederholung einer Silbe oder eines einzigen Wortes ist ein Merkmal der primitivsten Gesänge über ganz Nord-Amerika. [4]) Dieses gesellschaftliche Singen und Tanzen ist für den Indianer der höchste und fast einzige ästhetische Genuss, dem er sich mit Leidenschaft hingiebt, welche im Süden, auch zur Zeit der Entdeckung Amerikas,

---

1) Second Voyage to the Shores of the Polar Sea, London, 1823, ch. VIII.

2) Adair, History of the Amer. Indians, London, 1775, pp. 97, 110, 164; — H. H. Bancroft, Native Races of the Pacific States, New York, 1874, vol. I, p. 704—5; — Oviedo, Historia General y Natural de Indias, Madrid, 1851, parte I, lib. V, cap. I; — Torquemada, Monarchia Indiana, Madrid, 1723, tom II, lib. XIV, cap. XI; — Catlin, Letters and Notes etc., Phila, 1857, vol. I, p. 368; — Loskiel, Gesch. d. Mission d. evang. Brüder, Barby, 1879, S. 133; — Briefl. Mitth. an den Verf. von Herrn Y. Bonillas (Apaches) und Rev. M. Eells (Twanas, Clallams etc.); — unter den Irokesen in fast allen Tänzen [A-ō-doñ-wĕ]. — Es ist möglich, dass dieses Kreistanzen ursprünglich den Kreislauf der Sonne vorstellen sollte, da die Indianer Sonnenanbeter sind; diese Annahme wäre zugleich ein Grund für die Allgemeinheit des Kreistanzens. — Die Indianer am Milbank Sound (zw. 52°—6° nördl. Br., Pacific-Küste) halten die Sonne für einen glänzenden Mann, der um die Erde wandelt, während diese still steht; haben auch eine Vorstellung, in welcher die aufgehende Sonne von einem prachtvoll gekleideten Häuptling dargestellt wird (Dunn's Oregon Territory, Phila, 1845, p. 171—2).

3) Hierüber sind alle Schriftsteller einig.

4) Vergl. die Lieder X, XIX, XXVIII, XXIX, XXXII, XXXIX, XLII; — H. H. Bancroft vol. I, pp. 191, 281, 415; Dunn's Oregon Territory, p. 225—6.

1 *

durch geistige Getränke derart gesteigert wurde, dass die Feste manchmal in allgemeiner Betrunkenheit ihr Ende fanden; (bei religiösen Festen im Norden dagegen ist das Betragen der Mitwirkenden und Zuschauer ein sittlich musterhaftes). Die Abneigung des Indianers gegen Neuerungen, sein festes Beharren bei den durch die Zeit geheiligten Gebräuchen zeigen sich nirgends deutlicher als in Bezug auf Alles, was seine religiöse Musik betrifft; die Worte, die Melodien, ja sogar die kleinsten Geberden, werden wie ein unantastbares Heiligthum betrachtet, welches, von den Vorfahren kommend, den Nachkommen in unveränderter Gestalt überliefert werden muss; [1] wie im grossen Zaubertanze der Chippewas der Hauptgedanke immer wiederholt wird: »So machten es unsere Väter! nicht wahr, Brüder? die Väter haben uns das gelehrt! nicht wahr, Brüder? wir halten fest zu den guten alten Gebräuchen der Väter! das wollen wir, Brüder! [2] — Componirt man neue Lieder zu Ehren hervorragender Krieger, oder zum Andenken merkwürdiger Ereignisse, so weichen sie wenig vom allgemeinen Charakter der schon bekannten ab; [3] daher ist die musikalische Entwickelung jedenfalls eine sehr langsame gewesen, nicht aber wegen Mangel an Talent; die Indianer, unter dem Einfluss der Civilisation, machen oft rasche Fortschritte in der Musik. [4]

Die Indianergesänge überhaupt lassen sich, dem Charakter der Ceremonien gemäss, in denen sie gebraucht werden, in sieben Hauptklassen theilen. — 1. Cabbalistische, welche entweder in strenger Abgeschlossenheit nur von den in diese Mysterien Eingeweihten mit Tanz und roher Instrumentalbegleitung ausgeführt werden [vergl. »Schriftzeichen«]; oder

---

1) Torquemada, t. II, lib. XIV, cap. XI; — A-ō-doñ-wĕ hatte die Gesänge von seinem Vater gelernt; sein kleiner Sohn muss dieselben mit der peinlichsten Sorgfalt einstudiren; vergl. Rafinesque, vol. I, ch. V.

2) Briefl. Mitth. an den Verf. vom Rev. Isaac Baird, Odanah, Wis.

3) Torquemada, wie oben; — Oviedo, parte I, lib. V, cap. I.; — Der Verf. liess sich von verschiedenen Indianern solche »neue« Lieder vorsingen, die den »alten« sehr ähnlich waren.

4) Siehe besonders Torquemada, lib. XVII, cap. III.

von den Zauberärzten (medicine-men) zur Heilung kranker Personen, Verbannung böser Geister und dergleichen Künsten mehr angewendet werden. — 2. Religiöse: diesen Charakter tragen die meisten Gesänge, die zu besonderen Jahreszeiten regelmässig gesungen werden.[1] — 3. Historische [vergl. »Poesie«]. — 4. Kriegslieder. — 5. Trauergesänge. — 6. Liebeslieder. — 7. Lieder, welche bei geselligen Zusammenkünften jeder Art gesungen werden; diese haben häufig einen halb mystischen, halb religiösen Zug.

Alle Indianerstämme scheinen Gesänge zu haben, deren Ausbildung und Abwechselung mit dem Charakter der Völker übereinstimmen. Die wilden, kriegerischen Irokesen[2] besitzen weder historische Gesänge noch Liebeslieder, obgleich beide unter den sie umringenden Völkern gefunden werden. Unter den Irokesen nehmen die Frauen an dem Gesange keinen Antheil;[3] unter den Mexikanern dagegen, wo die Civilisation, und mit dieser auch die Musik, die grössten Fortschritte gemacht hatte, waren die Frauen in dieser Beziehung (sowie in vielen anderen) den Männern fast gleichberechtigt. Unter den Irokesen wieder werden die Tanzlieder von einer oder zwei Personen (oder einem Chor) ausgeführt, welche nicht tanzen; unter anderen Stämmen (namentlich den Mexikanern), singen die Tanzenden, und der Dirigent hat nur den Takt durch Paukenschläge anzugeben. Näher einzugehen in diese und andere Verschiedenheiten verbieten Mangel an Material und Ungenauigkeiten in dem vorhandenen; die Punkte, in welchen die Aufführungen der verschiedenen Völker mit einander übereinstimmen, scheinen übrigens zahlreicher und wichtiger zu sein.

---

1) Für Monatsfeste der Mexikaner s. Torquemada, lib. XII, cap. XXXIV.

2) Die »Fünf Nationen«: Senecas, Mohawks, Cayugas, Oneidas und Onondagas.

3) D. i. in den öffentlichen Festen.

---

## § 2. Poesie; Anfang und Entwickelung.

Einfache Naturlaute wie »he ya! he!« (XXVIII), oder
einige oft wiederholte, bedeutungslose[1]) Wörter wie »Ka-
noñ wi-yo« (IV), oder anscheinend unzusammenhängende
Wörter, wie »Freunde — Stein — bleiben immer fest — vorwärts!« sind mit den höher entwickelten Erscheinungen in
der Indianerpoesie innig verwandt, und dürften, in ihrer Ein-
fachheit und Natürlichkeit, als der Anfang und der Urquell
derselben betrachtet werden.[2]) Das freudige »he ya! he!« des
Comanche gehört nicht etwa diesem Volke allein, sondern
wird unter so weit auseinanderliegenden Völkern wie den Irokesen,[3]) Poncas[4]) und Twanas[5]) gefunden; das traurige
»Oh d-da d-da« (ach! ach!) der letztgenannten[6]) kommt wohl
in ähnlichen Gesängen anderer Indianernationen vor. Der
Uebergang von solchen blossen Ausrufungen zu einzelnen
Wörtern, und von diesen zu ganz kurzen Sätzen, ist ein leich-
ter, und im musikalischen Fortschritt überhaupt ein selbst-
verständlicher; der Wilde kann von solchen unvollständigen

---

1) A-ō-doñ-wĕ antwortete zuerst auf die Frage: »Haben diese
Worte irgend welche Bedeutung?« mit Bestimmtheit: »Nein«; nach
eifrigem Hin- und Herreden mit einem Freunde meinte er aber, dass
wi-yo soviel wie gut heisse; die Bedeutung von ka-noñ, sowie der
meisten Wörter im Weibertanze, sei ihm aber gänzlich unbekannt. —
Es kann sein, dass die Bedeutung der Worte mancher alten Lieder
von den Indianern vergessen worden, oder nur wenigen Eingeweihten
bekannt ist (die Wunderärzte haben z. B. eine besondere cabbalistische
Sprache). Sahagun (Hist. Univ. de las Cosas de N. España, in Lord
Kingsborough's Coll., London, 1831, vol. VII, S. 102) schreibt: »Los
cantares y psalmos que tiene compuestos, y se le cantan sin poderse
entender lo que en ellos se trata, mas de ellos que son naturales
y acostumbrados à este lenguage«. Vergl. Brasseur de Bourbourg,
Quatre Lettres sur le Mexique, Paris, 1869, 2me Lettre, § 5.

2) Vergl. Westphal, Elemente d. musik. Rhythmus, § 13: »Früheste
Anfänge der musischen Künste«.

3) Vergl. Lieder IV, V, VII.    4) XXXII (hi ye he!).

5) XXXIX, 19 (ha ya ha ya hi-hi-hi!). Civilisirte Völker haben
genau dieselben Ausrufungen.

6) XXXIX, 12.

Ausdrücken nur so lange ganz befriedigt werden, als seine geistige Bildung im Ganzen wenig entwickelt bleibt. Dass solche einfachen Gesänge zu gleicher Zeit mit anderen, weit höher ausgebildeten, noch bestehen können, ist nicht nur ein Beweis für die Beharrlichkeit des Indianercharakters, sondern zeigt ebenfalls, dass solche Lieder in innigster Verbindung mit seinem Empfindungsleben stehen; dass sie nicht gleich, wie etwas Abgenutztes und Veraltetes, zu verwerfen waren, sobald das Neue und (in musikalischer Beziehung) Vollkommenere entdeckt wurde, sondern immer noch, und hauptsächlich durch ihre Natürlichkeit, eine Anziehungskraft ausüben. Unter diesen einförmigen Liedern sind viele nicht nur durch den Gebrauch, sondern auch durch den Gegenstand geheiligt; der Name des Allerhöchsten wird in manchen religiösen Gesängen ausschliesslich, obgleich mit Variationen, gebraucht. [1] Die Gesänge haben oft, selbst in ihrer primitivsten Gestalt, eine dramatische Bestimmung; erst durch die Lebhaftigkeit der Mimik, durch die Sprache der Geberden, wird der eigentliche Sinn vieler kurzen Sätze klar. Auch ist in neuester Zeit entdeckt worden, dass in der Geberdensprache der Indianer ein weit tieferer Sinn liegt, als man bisher vermuthete; [2] es wird sogar angenommen, dass sie Gemeingut der verschiedensten wilden Indianervölker sei, von allen verstanden und unter einander gebraucht. [3] Indianer, welche kein Wort in der Sprache

---

1) Vergl. besonders Adair, Hist. of the Am. Indians; unter den Cherokees und verwandten Völkern waren die heiligen Silben Yo-he-wah (hebr. Je-ho-va); A. nennt die Indianer stets »die rothen Hebräer« (s. seine Argumente, S. 97, 121, 164 u. s. w.). — Die Huronen sangen dieselben Silben (Heriot's Travels, p. 82—3). — Die Nez-Percés brauchten die Silben »Ho-ha, ho-ha« in ihren gottesdienstlichen Gesängen (Dunn's Oregon Terr'y, p. 225—6.

2) Vergl. (für die Mexikaner) Brasseur, Quatre Lettres, 2me Lettre, § 7; 4me L., § 8 u. s. w.; seine Erklärung ist mindestens sehr originell, und, wie seine Ansichten überhaupt, von entschiedenem Interesse.

3) Lieut.-Col. Garrick Mallery's Collection of Gesture Signs and Signals of the N. A. Indians, Washington, Government Printing Office, 1880, enthält über 2000 solche Zeichen.

anderer verstehen, halten mit diesen stundenlange Unterredungen in dieser stummen Sprache, und können auf solche Weise die weitläufigsten Mittheilungen machen. Da ihm eine so mächtige Unterstützung, oder vielmehr Ergänzung seiner Worte zu Gebote steht, ist es ersichtlich, dass der Indianer weit weniger Wörter als der Civilisirte bedarf, um Alles, was in ihm und um ihn vorgeht, auszudrücken; in jenen kürzesten Sätzen geben die Worte nur einen festen Anhaltepunkt, um welchen er seine ganze Darstellungskunst[1]) in unbeschränkter Freiheit ausüben kann. In solchen Fällen, wo der darstellende Tänzer sich der Geberdensprache allein bedient (wie im Lied III der Notenbeilagen, in welchem die Worte von zwei, mitten im Kreise der Tanzenden sitzenden »Dirigenten« gesungen werden), ist die Wirkung, selbst dem in der Geberdensprache ununterrichteten Beobachter, eine überraschende. Die jungen Krieger, sich ganz den Gefühlen des Moments hingebend, führen die abenteuerlichsten Sprünge aus; sie werfen den Körper bald nach rechts oder nach links, bald vorwärts oder rückwärts mit erstaunlicher Heftigkeit; sich mit fletschenden Zähnen und schwarzen, feurigen, wildrollenden Augen Gesicht zu Gesicht angrinzend, drehen sie sich, wild aufjauchzend, im nächsten Augenblicke mit Blitzesschnelligkeit um, alle Bewegungen von den lebhaftesten Geberden der Arme und Hände begleitend; die Worte »Wolf rennt« finden in lebenden Bildern ihre vollste Auslegung; doch mitten im wildesten Getümmel kommt keiner aus dem Tact, welcher durch heftiges Stampfen mit den Füssen scharf markirt wird. — Bei einer wichtigen Unternehmung, wie einem nahe bevorstehenden Kriegszug, wo es gilt, den Zurückhaltenden Muth einzuflössen,

---

1) Diese hat unter manchen Indianernationen einen nicht unbedeutenden Grad der Fertigkeit erreicht. Vergl. Brasseur, Grammaire de la langue Quiché, Paris, 1862, Ballet - Drame de Rabinal - Achi; — Clavigero, Buch 7, Abschn. 43; — Acosta, lib. V, cap. XXIX; — H. H. Bancroft, vol. I, pp. 170, 199, 393; — Dunn's Oregon Terr'y, p. 171—2; — Loskiel, S. 133. — Die auffallende Aehnlichkeit mancher Vorstellungen wird Niemandem entgehen. Der Gebrauch, in vielen Festen, von geschnitzten Holzmasken, scheint ein allgemeiner zu sein.

bietet der Krieger seine ganzen Kräfte auf. Mit langsamen, schleichenden Schritten, als wollte er den Feind im nächsten Augenblicke überfallen, geht er, die Kriegsaxt (tomahawk, spr. -hōk) in der Hand, um den Kreis der versammelten Krieger herum, den Kriegsgesang (für den Irokesen ist dieser Nr. IX) mit männlicher Entschlossenheit singend; dann mit der Axt in die bemalte »Kriegspfoste« schlagend, erzählt er mit gehobener Stimme und kräftigem Ausdruck seine früheren glorreichen Thaten,[1]) und was er im bevorstehenden Zuge zu unternehmen gedenkt; durch seine Rede und den Applaus der anderen angefeuert, treten nun die Zaudernden in den Kreis, und singen denselben Gesang (ich gehe! ich gehe!) mit passenden Geberden, wodurch sie ihre Absicht, den Kriegszug mitzumachen, kund thun. — Das erste dieser beiden Beispiele zeigt die Beziehung der kürzeren Sätze zur äusseren Natur; das zweite, wie sie aus Ereignissen oder Handlungen entstehen können. Durch häufige Wiederholungen derselben Worte, welche oft stattfinden, kann nicht allein den Melodien mehr Abwechselung und grössere Länge gegeben werden, sondern es wird auch dem Darstellenden Gelegenheit geboten, nach Belieben die mannigfaltigsten Variationen, und dadurch seine eigene Geschicklichkeit, den Zuschauern vorzuführen; je wilder, desto naturgetreuer. Die Beziehung des Indianers zur Natur, sein Leben in und unmittelbare Berührung mit ihr, geben seinem Geiste die kräftigste und dauerndste Anregung; aus dieser nie versiegenden Quelle quillt ihm, in ewig wechselnden Formen, der Gedanken- und Empfindungsstoff entgegen, welcher einen grossen Theil seiner Gedichte ausmacht; und gerade in dieser Unmittelbarkeit der Wirkung und Empfindung liegt der Hauptreiz derselben. Seine Reden, sowohl wie seine poetischen Erzeugnisse, zeigen eine Fülle der schönsten, der Natur direct entliehenen Gleichnisse; ja, der Hauptunterschied zwischen der feierlichen Rede und der Poesie besteht darin, dass diese gelernt und gesungen, jene improvisirt und gespro-

---

1) Vergl. Loskiel, S. 135; hier singt der Krieger seine »Heldenthaten«, und sein Gesang wird von den andern begleitet, wie in IX zu sehen.

chen wird. Die natürliche Empfindungskraft wird durch den Aberglauben noch gesteigert; dem Indianerhäuptling ist es keine blosse rhetorische Figur wenn er den versammelten Kriegern zuruft: — »Wohl fühl' ich, dass eure Kriegsäxte nach Feindesblut dürsten, und dass eure treuen Pfeile ungeduldig streben, ihren Flug durch die Luft zu nehmen«; [1] er glaubt an Zauberpfeile und -Aexte, und dass in solchen leblosen Dingen ein geheime Lebenskraft liegt; wie er auch meint, die Thiere können ihn ganz gut verstehen, wenn er zu ihnen spricht. Die Poesie hat selten einen regelmässigen, metrischen Bau, und ist daher (soweit bis jetzt bekannt) grösstentheils einer gesungenen Prosa gleich. Einige Schriftsteller gehen so weit, dass sie behaupten, die wenigen uns bekannten Beispiele metrischer oder gereimter Verse seien eher das Resultat eines glücklichen Zufalles, als die Folge eines überlegten Versuchs. Die gegenwärtig vom Smithsonian Institute unternommenen Forschungen werden in wenigen Jahren mehr Licht auf dieses interessante Thema werfen; unterdessen ist Schreiber dieses entschieden der Meinung, dass bei der in den Melodien der Indianer häufig vorkommenden metrischen Eintheilung [2], die eine Folge eines regen rhythmischen Gefühls ist, ein Gleiches auch in der Poesie zu erwarten sei, und ebenfalls als eine Folge jenes rhythmischen Gefühls; nicht als eine zufällige Erscheinung, sondern als ein zwar nicht weit entwickelter, jedoch wirklicher Ordnungsversuch. [3] Solcher Klingklang

wie (XI):

> O-la-ko-ta
> Ku-wa-ki-ya | pe!

oder (XXXI):

> A ki le
> Li wañ pe

oder (XIV):

---

1) Adair, S. 61.     2) Vergl. »Rhythmus«.

3) Diese Ansicht findet eine überraschende Bestätigung in einem Bericht (im Boston Herald für d. 17. Juni 1881) über die Forschungen des Herrn F. H. Cushing unter den Zuñis, worin es heisst: »In rhyme and rhythm the poetry is as perfect as the work of our most finished lyrists«.

Ko la ta ku ya ka pe lo
O ki ci ze ima tan can ye lo
E ha ka lesh le han̄ wa on̄ we lo
E ye ye ye lo

wird dem Ohr des Wilden ebenso angenehm sein, wie kleinen
Kindern die alten Wiegenlieder; solche Lieder sind auch an
und für sich als Beweismittel nicht wichtig; erst im Zusammenhang mit anderen, höher entwickelten, gewinnen sie Bedeutung. Auf einer höheren Stufe stehen folgende drei Lieder:

### 1. Serenade (Sioux, XII).

Shicé, shicé shanté, mashicä,
Shicé lakà shicé napé, mayúsä;
   Shicé wanci, yakéshni,
   Shicé shanté, mashicä,
  Shicé lakà shicé napé, mayúsä.
(Uebersetzung in den Notenbeilagen.)

### 2. Das Erdbeben.[1]

Tu-wip′ pu-a, tu-wip pu-a
  A-vwim̄-pai-ar-ru-wip′ pu-a
Tu-rá-gu-ok, tu-rá-gu-ok
  Kai-vwa mu-tú-rai-ka-nok.
(In jenem Land, in jenem Land
  In jenem glänzenden Land
Weit von hier, weit von hier
  Bebte der Berg vor Schmerzen.)

### 3. Das Paradoxon.

Wi-giv′-a ka.ri-′ri
  Yú-ga-kai-mai-u-uk
  Yú-ga-kai-mai-u-uk
Ma-mum̄-pa-ri-tum-pa.
(Der Kamm des Berges
  Bleibt ewig da,
  Bleibt ewig da,
Doch fallen stets Felsen.)

---

1) Dieses Lied, sowie das nächstfolgende, sind Prof. J. W. Powell's
»Report of Explor. in 1873 of the Colorado [Fluss] of the West« (Smiths.
Inst.) entnommen.

Die beiden letzten Lieder, von einem Volke, dessen Vorfahren in aller Wahrscheinlichkeit in näheren Beziehungen zu den Mexikanern standen, haben für uns ein doppeltes Interesse; alle drei zeigen etwas mehr, als eine blos zufällige Zusammenstellung der Wörter. Noch bedeutender sind die historischen Gesänge der »Wapahani« oder White River Indianer; der Uebersetzer[1]) hält dieselben, in ihrer jetzigen Gestalt, für »eine blose Verkürzung vollständigerer Annalen, welche jetzt wahrscheinlich verloren gegangen«. Der nachstehende Theil wird wegen seines unstreitbar metrischen Charakters angeführt; er wurde jedenfalls theilweise wegen der Erleichterung für's Gedächtniss, die eine solche Regelmässigkeit gewährt, in dieser Form verfasst. Das hier Gegebene fängt mit dem 13. Liede des 3. Gesanges an.

13. Amakolen
Nallahemen
Agunuken
Powasinep
Wapasinep
Akomenep

14. Wihlamok kicholen luchundi
Wematan akomen luchundi.

15. Witéhen wémiluen
Wémaken nihillen.

16. Nguttichin Lowaniwi
Nguttichin Wapaniwi.
Agamunk topanpek
Wulliton épannek

17. Wulélémil W'shakuppek
Wémopannek hakhsinipek
Kitahikan pokhakhopek

18. Tellenchen kittapaki nillawi
Wémoltin gutikuni nillawi

---

1) Rafinesque, in The Amer. Nations, vol. I, ch. V. — Eine engl. Uebers. dieser 3 histor. Gesänge ist im Nachtrage zu Brasseur's »Quatre Lettres sur le Mexique« zu finden; der erste und zweite Gesang, mit Copien der Indianerzeichnungen, in Beach's Indian Miscellany, Albany, N. Y., 1877.

Akomen wapanaki nillawi
Ponskan-ponskan wémuvi Olini.

19. Lowanapi Wapanapi Shawanapi
Lanéwapi Tamakwapi Tuméwapi
Elowapi Powatipi Wilawapi
Okwisapi Danisapi Allumapi.

20. Wemipayat gunéyunga Shinaking
Wunkénapi chanelendam payaking
Allowélendam kowiyey Tulpaking.

(Uebersetzung.

13. — Während unsere Vorfahren immer auf dem Wasser fuhren, sahen sie im Osten, dass das Schlangenland hell und reich war.

14. — Der Hauptbiber Wihlamok [1]) und der Grosse-Vogel Kicholen sagten allen, gehen wir nach der Schlangeninsel Akomen.

15. — Kommt ihr mit uns, so vertilgen wir das ganze Schlangenvolk.

16. — Alle hiermit einverstanden, Die-vom-Norden und Die-vom-Westen, gingen über das Wasser des gefrornen Meeres, um das Land zu nehmen.

17. — Es war merkwürdig, als sie alle über das glatte, dunkle Wasser des gefrornen Meeres gingen, beim Durchgang von der Schlangensee in das grosse Meer.

18. — Es waren zehntausend im Dunkeln, die alle fortgehèn in einer einzigen Nacht im Dunkeln, nach der Schlangeninsel des östlichen Landes Wapanaki, zu Fuss das ganze Volk.

19. — Sie waren das männliche Norden, das männliche Osten, das männliche Süden; mit männlichem Adler, männlichem Biber, männlichem Wolf; mit männlichem Jäger, männlichem Priester, männlichem Reichen; mit männlichem Weib [2]), männlicher Tochter, männlichem Hund.

---

1) Name eines Häuptlings (Anm. d. Verf.).

2) Die Bezeichnung »männlich« wird wahrscheinlich wie »muthig« oder »tapfer« gebraucht für diejenigen, welche diesen gefahrvollen Uebergang wagten; der Indianer lobt seine eigenen Thaten gern.

20. — Alle dorthin gekommen, bleiben sie im Föhrenlande Shinaking. Aber Die-vom-Westen, den Uebergang zweifelhaft findend, zogen es vor, im alten Schildkrötenland zu bleiben.) —

Ueber die Verbreitung solcher, für die Geschichte des Indianers höchst wichtigen Gesänge, ist wenig Bestimmtes bekannt. Die Entdeckungsreisen der Spanier zeigten, dass die Ureinwohner von Hayti, Cuba, [1]) Yucatan, [2]) Mexiko [3]) und einem Theil von Central-Amerika [4]) historische Gesänge besassen. Nach Rafinesque [5]) hatten die Shawanis, die Illinois und fast jede Linapi Nation ebenfalls solche Gesänge, die man die eigentlich nationalen nennen kann.

---

### § 3. Vocalisation und Vortrag.

In diesem kurzen Paragraphen sollen nur die in den Liedern I bis incl. XXXII vorkommenden Eigenthümlichkeiten der Vocalisation uud Vortragsweise besprochen werden.

**a. Consonanten.** — B, d, f, h, k, l, m, n, p, r und t werden wie im deutschen ausgesprochen; c = tsch; g ist stets hart; ħ ist ein rauher Kehllaut; j wie im französischen Wort je; n̄ wie im franz. noñ; s = ss; sh = sch; w und y fast wie u resp. i, nur dass zu ihrer richtigen Aussprache eine etwas kräftigere Zusammenziehung der Lippen und Kehle, als zu der jener einfachen Vocale, gehört; z wie im französischen zèle.

**b. Vocale.** — Das a wird in den Gesängen der Senecas wie a in Vater ausgesprochen; in denen der Iowas und Kiowas hat es oft, wenn gesungen, eine dunklere Farbe, zwischen a und dem italienischen ō, obgleich beim Sprechen diese Eigenthümlichkeit weniger bemerkbar ist; in den übrigen Liedern wie unter den Senecas. Das ă ist das französische und englische

---

1) Oviedo, parte I, lib. V, cap. I.
2) Cogolludo, Hist. de Yucatan, lib. IV, cap. V, ap Landa.
3) Veytia, Historia Antigua de Mejico, Madrid, 1836, lib. III, cap. VII; — Torquemada, lib. XII, cap. XXXIV, auch lib. II, c. XLI.
4) Brasseur; H. H. Bancroft.    5) Wie oben.

kurze *a* (*patte, pat*); mit *n̄* verbunden wie *ain* in *pain*. Das *ä*
lautet wie das deutsche *ä*. *E* ist fast immer dem französischen *é*
gleich (= *ee* in *See*), wenn gesungen zuweilen etwas breiter; nur
bei einem raschen Uebergang, oder bei Staccato-Stellen, ist es
kurz.

Das *i* ist stets lang (= *ie* in *Kiel*). Das *o*, mit *n̄* verbunden,
lautet wie im französischen *non;* *ō* ist das breite italienische *o;*
sonst hat dieser Vocal den Laut von *oo* in *Boot*, schnelle Ueber-
gänge und Staccato-Stellen ausgenommen, in welchen es dem
*o* in *soll* gleicht. *U* wie *u* in *Hut*. Die Intonation sämmtlicher
Vocale ist eine volle, sich etwas zum Breiten neigende, sonst
aber rein und deutlich; hierdurch wird die Wirksamkeit der
Gesänge bedeutend erhöht. Die meisten Silben endigen auf
Vocale, oder auf solche Consonanten wie *n* und *n̄*, welche
einen leichten Uebergang von einer Tonstufe zur andern ver-
mitteln; dies verleiht den Liedern einen wohlklingenden, fliess-
senden Charakter, ohne dass der streng fortschreitende Rhythmus ihnen gestattet, schmelzend zu werden. Die Anfangscon-
sonanten werden bisweilen von den sie begleitenden Vocalen
scharf abgesondert ausgestossen, wie in XVI und XVII (*t'o*),
oder im XXX (*g'li, t'eon̄*). Die Silben werden häufig gerade
ihres Wohllauts wegen gewählt, »um ein gutes Lied zu machen«
sagte der Seneca A-ō-don̄-wĕ. (Beispiele hiervon sind die beiden Lieder des Weibertanzes IV und V.) Bedeutungslose Silben
werden in einigen Fällen, des Wohlklangs wegen, solchen
Versen angehängt, in denen die Bedeutung der übrigen Wörter
bekannt, und durch diese Zuthat keineswegs geändert wird.[1]
Eine Verdoppelung des Vocals findet zuweilen statt, wenn er
ausnahmsweise scharf betont werden soll (im III. Lied *ni-i*;
IV. *a-a*).

**c. Der Umfang der Stimme** des Indianers ist, so weit die
Erfahrung des Verfassers reicht, nicht kleiner als der des
Weissen, d. h. natürlich beide im ungeschulten Zustande ver-

---

1) Unter den Dakotas (Sioux) vgl. Riggs, Grammar and Dictionary of
the Dakota Language, (Vol. IV of Smiths. Cont. to Knowledge) Introduction. Vgl. die Lieder XIII bis XVIII, in welchen die Silben »ye! ye!
ye!« bloss euphonische sind. (Briefl. Mittheil. von Rev. T. L. Riggs.)

glichen. (Dies hat jedoch nur auf Männer Bezug.) Die Lieder
wurden fast ohne Ausnahme in hoher (Bariton) Lage gesungen;
die meisten Ausführenden besassen aber die Fähigkeit bis zum
grossen $F$ hinab mit vollkräftiger Stimme zu singen; der Verfasser hat keinen gehört der das tenor $f'$ nicht mit Leichtigkeit
nehmen könnte. Ein Chor von siebzehn jungen Männern sangen
das Lied Nr. IV einen ganzen Ton höher als es in den Notenbeilagen angegeben ist, und die höheren Töne nicht etwa falsetto, sondern mit voller Bruststimme. Der Umfang der männ-
lichen Stimme wäre durchschnittlich auf zwei Octaven zu
setzen; vom grossen $F$ bis zum tenor $f'$; oder vom grossen $A$
bis zum tenor $a'$.

    **d. Vortragsweise.** Diese ist, dem Charakter der Poesie und
der Melodien gemäss, eine höchst n a i v e; für crescendo und de-
crescendo, accelerando und ritardando, scheinen die Sänger
kein Bedürfniss zu empfinden; was die Melodien hierdurch für
das sentimentale Gefühl verlieren, gewinnen sie durch ihre natürliche Frische und das augenscheinliche Vergnügen, welches
ihr Vortrag dem Indianer gewährt. Ueber die Qualität der
Stimmen lässt sich nicht viel sagen; der Verfasser hat sie nicht
unangenehmer gefunden als die der (überhaupt) ungebildeten
Weissen; im Gegentheil, da unter den Indianern alle eine gewisse Uebung im Singen haben, und die Intervalle sehr sicher
und rein genommen werden, war der Eindruck bei diesen Aufführungen eher als ein angenehmer zu bezeichnen; einige, die
in ihrer Art und Weise am meisten geübten Sänger, hatten
wirklich weiche, wohlklingende Stimmen. Die Sicherheit der
Intonation und des rhythmischen Gefühls, zusammen mit der
vollen Hingebung aller Mitwirkenden, sind die Hauptvorzüge
ihrer Vortragsweise. [1]

    **e. Vortragsmanieren und Verzierungen.** Von diesen letz-
teren wird der u n v e r ä n d e r l i c h  k u r z e  Vorschlag am

---

    1) Bis zu einer Schule der Stimme (im europäischen Sinne) haben
es die Indianer nie gebracht; die Spanier fanden das Singen der Mexikaner rauh und unangenehm, obgleich diese später, unter spanischer
Leitung, Ausgezeichnetes leisteten (Torquemada, lib. XVII, cap. III).

häufigsten gebraucht, und stets scharf accentuirt; folgendes Beispiel ist dem Liede Nr. III entnommen:

Der Nachschlag kommt nicht selten, obgleich nicht so oft wie jener Vorschlag zur Anwendung, das Beispiel ist aus demselben Liede:

Das einzige Beispiel eines Doppelvorschlags findet man ebenfalls in III:

Der absteigende Schleifer (der aufsteigende kommt nicht vor) ist im XIV. Lied zu finden:

die kleinen Noten werden nicht einzeln und deutlich betont, sondern rasch mit einem Zuge, ungefähr wie bei uns ein schlechter Sänger, anstatt ein Intervall rein zu nehmen, beim unsicheren Uebergange die Zwischentöne undeutlich hören lässt, nur dass dies in den Indianergesängen mit Absicht und folglich mit mehr Deutlichkeit geschieht (Portamento); der Schleifer in Nr. X wird wie ein Jauchzer ausgeführt. Ein Knurren oder Summen, welches durch das Schliessen der Zähne bewerkstelligt wird, hat manchmal einen merkwürdigen Effect, wie z. B. im XIV. Lied (Scalptanz), 8. und 9. Tact, das plötzlich eintretende *gis* und der schleifende Uebergang zu *e* wirklich schaudererregend wirkten. Der Schleifer und das Knurren sind als charakteristisch wilde Vortragsmanieren zu bezeichnen.

2

## § 4. Tonart.

In diesem Paragraphen, sowie in den beiden folgenden, werden nur die Lieder I bis incl. XXXII einer eingehenden Analyse unterworfen; die übrigen werden nur zum Zweck des Vergleichs gebraucht.

Jene zwei und dreissig Lieder wurden mit einer Ausnahme (IX) unisono gesungen, gleichviel ob von Männer- oder Weiberstimmen, oder, wie in einigen Fällen (z. B. XXXI und XXXII), von beiden vereinigt gesungen. Die überwiegende Mehrzahl der Indianergesänge überhaupt trägt denselben Charakter; [1] mehrstimmige Gesänge kommen selten vor und nach den wenigen Beschreibungen solcher Fälle zu schliessen, wird die harmonische Gestaltung solcher mehrstimmigen Gesänge, bei der Wiederholung nach Willkür der Sänger derart verändert, dass die mehr oder weniger gut harmonirenden Begleitungsstimmen kein festes harmonisches Gefühl zeigen. Selbst die Mexikaner kannten den polyphonischen Gesang nicht, [2] obgleich bei diesen die Stimmen zuweilen von harmonirenden Instrumenten begleitet wurden. Eine solche Begleitung wird unter den wilden Indianern nicht gefunden; [3] ein Instrument wie die griechische Lyra, welche, selbst in ihrer unvollkommensten Gestalt, durch das Zusammenklingen und richtige Stimmen der Saiten einen mächtigen Einfluss auf die Ausbildung des harmonischen Gefühls ausübte, war jenen so-

---

[1] Torquemada, lib. II, cap. LXXXVIII (Mexiko); Oviedo, p. I, l. V, c. I (Hayti); H. H. Bancroft, p. 281, Foot-note (Nez-Percés); B rfl Mitth. a. d. Verf. vom Rev. M. Eells (Twanas, Clallams, Chemakums); Rev. E. Vetromile (Micmacs etc.); J. Bonillas (Apaches), Rev. Isaac Baird (Chippewas); Henry D. Wireman (Indianer in Montana). — Unter den Irokesen, Dakotas, Iowas, Kiowas, Poncas und Comanches, mündliche Mittheilungen a. d. Verf. von den Indianern.

[2] Torquemada, wie oben.

[3] Die Pueblo Indianer, sowie die Apaches und Comanches, welche drei Stämme sich unweit der mexikan. Grenze aufhalten, sollen Ausnahmen sein; ob ihre Begleitung wirklich eine harmonirende, und ob sie originell oder den Weissen oder den Azteken entlehnt worden, ist dem Verf. nicht bekannt.

wohl wie diesen unbekannt. Der wilde Indianer ist dennoch in
der primitiven Ausübung seiner Kunst so weit vorgeschritten,
dass sein Ohr die einfachen tonischen Verhältnisse in der diatonischen Tonleiter erkennt, und dass er daher die meisten
Intervalle in derselben rein und sicher singen kann. Nun entsteht die Frage, ob in diesen Melodien eine feste, sowohl vom
Indianer wie vom Civilisirten anerkannte Basis, ein Grundton,
vorhanden, von welchen ausgehend der Musiker den Charakter der Tonarten bestimmen und die Intervalle benennen kann.
Ueber den Standpunkt des Indianers giebt uns das IX. Lied
einigen Aufschluss; hier erscheint das vom Chor der Krieger
gesungene *f* als ein mit vollem und einstimmigem Bewusstsein
gewählter Grundton; [1]) das Ohr des Musikers würde denselben
Ton aus den unbegleiteten melodischen Folgen [2]) als Grundton
annehmen, wäre aber von dessen monotoner Wiederholung,
die auf andere, latente Harmonien (im 2. und 3., sowie im 11.
und 12. Tact, der Dominantseptimenaccord) keine Rücksicht
nimmt, durchaus nicht befriedigt. Ein weiteres Beispiel der
bewussten Wahl eines Grundtons findet man im Danksagungslied, § 7, 3., wo der Führer die Melodie singt, und der Chor
immer mit dem Grundton *f* antwortet. Beide Lieder sind von
den Irokesen; für diesen Stamm darf man mit Sicherheit annehmen, dass die Sänger die Existenz eines Grundtons in ihren
Melodien anerkennen; diese Annahme wird durch eine auch
nur oberflächliche Betrachtung der Lieder I bis incl. VIII noch
bekräftigt und lässt sich ohne Bedenken auf die anderen, ohne-
hin in anderen Beziehungen ebensoweit oder weiter entwickelten, durch ihre Gesänge hier vertretenen Völker übertragen.

---

1) Gesänge mit einer ähnlichen Begleitung auf dem Grundtone
hat man auch unter den Delawaren und den mit ihnen alliirten Nationen
(Loskiel, S. 134) unter den »Socs und Šous« (Briefl. Mitth. a. d. Verf.
vom Dr. A. C. Garratt), sowie unter den Twanas u. s. w. (Rev. M. Eells
in Amer. Antiquarian, April, Mai, Juni 1879) gehört. Dieses Lied (IX)
wurde schon Mitte des vorigen Jahrh. unter den Mohawks (Irokesen)
gehört. (Mc Knight, Our Western Border, p. 77—9).
2) Ueber das Wesentliche in den melodischen Folgen wird im
folgenden Abschnitte ausführlich gesprochen.

2*

Wie weit das harmonische Gefühl des Indianers reicht; welche begleitenden Töne, a u s s e r d e m G r u n d t o n e, seinem inneren Sinne vorschweben mögen, kann nicht mit Gewissheit gesagt werden. Da er aber, 1) zu den übrigen Gesängen (ausser IX) keine Vocalbegleitung braucht, 2) überhaupt zu keinen Gesängen eine harmonirende Instrumentalbegleitung geschaffen, obgleich, wie bei den Irokesen, seine Pauke einen bestimmten, leicht zu erkennenden Ton hat und ihm auch ein Flageolet zu Gebote steht, 3) in den obenerwähnten Fällen sich nur des Grundtons bedient, und zwar in solchen Stellen, wo dem musikalisch gebildeten Ohr eine Abwechselung geboten erscheint, und endlich 4) weil das Singen in unisono, ohne irgend welche harmonische Vocal- oder Instrumentalbegleitung, ein wesentliches Merkmal der Indianergesänge im allgemeinen und der in den Notenbeilagen angegebenen im besonderen ist, — so wird eine jede Melodie, in welcher keine zufälligen Versetzungszeichen (i. e. solche, die durch andere aufgehoben werden) vorkommen, in dem Sinne analysirt, als bewegte sie sich stets in einer und derselben Tonart, also ohne Grundtonwechsel. Nach Ansicht des Verfassers ist diesen Melodien keine im modernen Style modulirte harmonische Begleitung anzupassen; so wird zwar der subjectiven Fantasie (Willkür?) wenig Spielraum gelassen, desto mehr aber einer vorurtheilsfreien, objectiven Betrachtung; mit diesem Vorbehalt darf man nach Belieben nach l a t e n t e n H a r m o n i e n suchen.

In den meisten Fällen ist der Grundton[1]) unschwer zu bestimmen, besonders in solchen, wo Sext und Septime, welche den Melodien oft eine eigenthümliche Färbung verleihen, nicht vorhanden sind. Solche Melodien sind: I, mit Grundton *g*; III, Grundton *a*; IV, Grundton *g*; IX, Grundton *f*; XI, Grundton *c*; XX, Grundton *f*; XXIV und XXV, Grundton *c*; XXVI, Grundton *b*; XXVIII, Grundton *g*; und XXXI, mit Grundton *d*. Diese Melodien, mit Ausnahme von IX nnd XX, denen die Terz fehlt, kann man schlechthin als Dur bez. Moll bezeichnen, da die kleine Secunde nicht vorkommt, und Quarte

---

1) Vergl. »Tabelle der Tonstufen«.

und Quinte stets rein gesungen werden. In den weniger einfachen Fällen wird der Grundton bestimmt, entweder durch die melodischen Folgen, oder den melodischen Accent, oder durch diese beiden zusammen.

**a.** Die melodischen Folgen sind in folgenden Melodien, in der Wahl des Grundtons, das eigentlich Bestimmende: II, Grundton $a$, wo die Folge $e'\ c'\ a\ e'\ c'\ a\ e$[1]) die bestimmende bleibt, trotz der wiederholten Betonung des, sich zu $e$ als kleine Terz, zu $a$ als kleine Septime verhaltenden $g$, welches sich immer wieder zur Tonica wendet, entweder direct oder durch die Folgen $g\ h\ e'\ c'\ a$ (10. Tact) und $g\ e'\ a\ (e')$ (Schluss); VIII, Grundton $c$, wo die Folgen $e'\ c'$ (1. und 2. Tact), $c'\ g$ (4. Tact) und $e\ c'\ c'\ e$ (7. und 8. Tact) dem Ganzen den Charakter einer Durtonart geben, der durch die Folge $e\ g$ und $g\ e$ (10. und 11. Tact) und die wiederholte Betonung des $e$ am Schluss keine Veränderung erleidet; XV, Grundton $c'$, in welcher die Folge $g'\ f'\ d'\ c'$ (3. und 4. Tact), wie die ähnliche Folge in IX (2., 3. und 4. Tact) zusammen mit $g\ c'$ (11. Tact), wo die Quinte sich zum Grundton wendet, für die Wahl der Tonica maassgebend ist; ferner in VII und XII, Grundton $c'$; XIV, Grundton $a$; XVIII, Grundton $g$; XIX, Grundton $e'$; XXI, Grundton $c'$; XXVII, Grundton $d'$; und XXX, Grundton $g$.

**b.** Durch den melodischen Accent wird der Grundton in folgenden Melodien bestimmt: XVI und XVII, mit Grundton $d$, welches in beiden sich durch die wiederholte Betonung am Schluss bemerkbar macht; in diesen beiden Beispielen genügen die melodischen Folgen nicht, um den Grundton mit Gewissheit zu bezeichnen; dass beide mit der Secunde anfangen, ist auffallend, in XI aber, wo der Grundton ohne Zweifel $c$ ist, ist dies auch der Fall (vergl. XXXI, 10. Tact); — und XXXII, Grundton $g$; hier wäre man vielleicht im Anfange (4., 5. und 6. Tact) geneigt, das $c'$ als eine durch die melodischen Folgen bezeichnete Tonica, zu wählen; dieses $c'$ scheint aber nicht,

---

1) In folgenden Beispielen wird die wirkliche Tonhöhe, welche in den im G-Schlüssel notirten Melodien eine Octave tiefer als die notirte ist, angegeben.

wie in anderen Melodien der Grundton, einen festen Anhaltepunkt zu bieten, sondern wird nur vorübergehend gebraucht.

**c.** Durch die Verbindung des Accents mit den melodischen
Folgen wird der Grundton bestimmt in: XIII, Grundton *e*;
XXII, Grundton *c'*; XXIII, Grundton *b*; und XXIX, Grundton *es*; im letzten Beispiele fällt der Accent auf *g, es* und *b* in
der auffallendsten Weise, wodurch die übrigen Töne als Durch-
gangsnoten erscheinen, jene somit die Bedeutung des Haupt-
oder tonischen Accords haben; der Schluss auf der Sext zeigt
eine merkwürdige Abweichung von dem in den anderen Melodien zu bemerkenden Gebrauch.

Nachdem der Grundton einer jeden Melodie festgesetzt
worden, kann zur Untersuchung der Intervallenverhältnisse
und zur Benennung der Tonarten geschritten werden. Ein Blick
auf die am Schlusse beigegebene »Tabelle der Intervalle« wird
zeigen, dass alle sieben Stufen der diatonischen Tonleiter nur
selten in e i n e r dieser kurzen Melodien gefunden werden, dass
nicht allein der G r u n d t o n, sondern auch die Q u i n t e, in
jeder Melodie[1]) vorkommt, und in allen re in gesungen wird;
die T e r z findet man in fünfundzwanzig Melodien, in einund-
zwanzig die g r o s s e und in vier die k l e i n e; die Q u a r t e in
zweiundzwanzig Melodien und, mit einer Ausnahme, die re ine;
die Sext wird in fünfzehn Melodien gefunden und zwar stets
die g r o s s e; die S e p t i m e erscheint in acht Melodien, in fünf
als die k l e i n e, in zwei als die g r o s s e, und in einer kommen
beide vor.

Ueber das harmonische Wesen der Indianergesänge haben
sich in weiten Kreisen die irrthümlichsten Meinungen verbrei-
tet. Einerseits wird behauptet, es sei unmöglich, ihrer harmonischen und rhythmischen Abweichungen vom modernen Tonsystem wegen, die Melodien in unserer Notenschrift wiederzugeben, andererseits meint man, dass die Tonarten in ihrer Zahl
und ihren Intervallenverhältnissen mit denen der Perser und
Indier verglichen werden könnten. Was die erste Ansicht betrifft, so sei nur bemerkt, dass der Verfasser sich nicht damit be-

---

1) **Nr. X**, als m o n o t o n natürlich ausgenommen.

gnügte, sich sämmtliche Lieder von I bis incl. XXXII vorsingen zu lassen, sondern er hat dieselben, sobald er sie einige Mal gehört hatte, mit den Indianern zusammen durchgesungen; durch dieses Verfahren wäre eine wesentliche Abweichung von unseren Tonverhältnissen sehr leicht zu erkennen gewesen; der Verfasser hat sich im Gegentheil überzeugt, dass die Indianer s e h r   r e i n (wie das Wort unter Musikern gebraucht wird) singen. [Vergl. auch »Rhythmus«.] — Gegen die zweite Ansicht lässt sich Folgendes einwenden: 1) Der seltene Gebrauch des Halbtonschritts und die völlige Vermeidung eines kleineren, dies und 2) die äusserst spärliche Anwendung zufälliger Versetzungszeichen und 3) das hieraus entspringende rein diatonische Gepräge der grossen Mehrzahl der Melodien macht die Zahl der Tonarten zu einer verhältnissmässig beschränkten; d i e s e Tonarten sind übrigens die Frucht einer n a t ü r l i c h e n, u n g ek ü n s t e l t e n   E n t w i c k e l u n g, die jener orientalischen Völker eines t h e o r e t i s c h - p e d a n t i s c h e n, p o m p h a ft e n   S y s t e m s. — Wollte man, wenn in einer oder der anderen Melodie diese oder jene Stufe der Tonleiter fehlt, in dieser Unvollständigkeit die Ursache zur Benennung einer neuen Scala oder Tonleiter finden, so wäre dadurch die Zahl der Tonarten in einer unzweckmässigen Weise vermehrt, weil der Indianer zwar gewisse m e l o d i s c h e   F o l g e n, jedoch k e i n e   b e s o nd e r e   T o n s t u f e in der diatonischen Tonleiter zu vermeiden scheint. Weit eher wären diese Scalen in Bezug auf die Stellung des Halbtonschritts, mit denen der Griechen in der Zeit vor Aristoxenos (um 350 v. Chr.) zu vergleichen. Diese Tonarten der »Alten« waren folgende: [1]

1. Mixolydisch $= H\,c\,d\,e\,f\,g\,a\,h$
2. Lydisch $= c\,d\,e\,f\,g\,a\,h\,c'$
3. Phrygisch $= d\,e\,f\,g\,a\,h\,c'\,d'$
4. Dorisch $= e\,f\,g\,a\,h\,c'\,d'\,e'$
5. Hypolydisch $= f\,g\,a\,h\,c'\,d'\,e'\,f'$

---

[1] Paul, Absolute Harmonik der Griechen, Leipzig, 1866. S. 15. — Diese Scalen sind sowohl von den gleichnamigen Transpositionsscalen des Aristoxenos, wie von den Tonarten des 16. Jahrh., zu unterscheiden.

6. Hypophrygisch $= g\ a\ h\ c\ d'\ e'\ f'\ g'$
7. Hypodorisch $= a\ h\ c'\ d'\ e'\ f'\ g'\ a'$
   oder Lokrisch $= A\ H\ c\ d\ e\ f\ g\ a.$

Da in keiner der vorliegenden Melodien die kleine Secunde oder die verminderte Quinte vorkommt, so ist anzunehmen, dass unter den Indianern die Mixolydische Tonart selten oder gar nicht gebraucht wird; die Lokrische Tonart hat dieselben Intervallenverhältnisse wie die Hypodorische. mit Ausschluss der Mixolydischen und Hypodorischen können die »Tonarten der Alten« in folgenden zwei Octaven der diatonischen Tonleiter wiedergegeben werden:

$$c\ d\ e\ f\ g\ a\ h\ c'\ d'\ e'\ f'\ g'\ a'\ h'\ c''$$

indem ein jeder der sechs Anfangstöne der Reihe nach als Ausgangspunkt oder Grundton einer neuen Tonart oder »Octavengattung« gesetzt wird; die Bogen zeigen die Stellung des Halbtons.

Die Lydische Tonart findet in VII eine in allen Intervallen passende Vertreterin, da diese wie jene die grosse Secunde, grosse Terz, reine Quarte, reine Quinte, grosse Sext und grosse Septime hat. [1]

Die Phrygische Tonart hat grosse Secunde, kleine Terz, reine Quarte, reine Quinte, grosse Sext und kleine Septime; unter den ersten zweiunddreissig Melodien befindet sich keine, in welcher alle Tonstufen dieser Scala gefunden werden, in drei Beispielen aber (II, XIV und XVII) sind die kleine Terz und kleine Septime zu finden, in II fehlen nur die Quarte (die mit einer Ausnahme stets rein gesungen wird) und die Sext (welche immer gross ist), in XIV sind die Secunde (sonst

---

[1] Vergl. »Kriegslied der Chippewas« (XXXIII). — Erwähnenswerth ist die Thatsache, dass die Scala sa der Hindus nicht nur dieselben tonischen Verhältnisse hatte, sondern auch in solchen Gesängen, die von »heroischer Liebe und Tapferkeit« handelten, gebraucht wurde. (Siehe Jones, On the Musical Modes of the Hindus, in vol. I. of Works, London, 1799.) — »Im 16. Jahrhundert glaubte man, dass dieser Modus (der Jonische = Alt-Lydische], hauptsächlich zur Erzeugung einer freudigen Stimmung geeignet wäre«. Paul, Absol. Harm. der Griechen, S. 41.

stets gross) und die Sext nicht vorhanden, in XVII fehlt nur
die Sext, überdies bewegen sich XXXVII und XXXVIII in
dieser Tonart, daher erscheint die Annahme, dass die Phrygische Tonart keine seltene Erscheinung in der Indianermusik
sein dürfte, als eine berechtigte,[1]) besonders weil die grosse Sext
und kleine Septime von den Indianern mit Vorliebe gewählt
werden. [Vergl. »Tabelle der Intervalle«.]

Die Dorische Tonart hat die kleine Secunde und kommt
unter diesen Melodien nicht vor.

Die Hypolydische Tonart wird nicht vollständig gefunden; in XXIII tritt die übermässige Quarte einmal auf,
wird aber gleich darnach von der reinen verdrängt. (Beim
flüchtigen Gebrauch eines zufälligen Versetzungszeichens wie
hier und auch in XIV, wo die grosse Septime einmal erscheint,
ist kein Wechsel im Grundton ersichtlich; im ersten Falle bleibt
er *b*, im zweiten *a*; die Tonart erleidet aber durch die Ver-
schiebung des Halbtonintervalls eine wesentliche Veränderung; durch den vorübergehenden Gebrauch der übermässigen
Quarte kommt das Klagende im Liede zu bestimmterem Ausdruck; es war nicht zu verkennen, dass die Indianer die durch
solche Veränderung erzielte erhöhte Wirkung fühlten und be-
absichtigten.)

Die Hypophrygische Tonart mit grosser Secunde.
grosser Terz, reiner Quarte und Quinte, grosser Sext und
kleiner Septime, ist in zwei Beispielen (V und XV) vollständig zu finden; in dieser Tonart oder in der Lydischen scheinen
die meisten Melodien mit grosser Terz sich zu bewegen.

Die Hypodorische Tonart, mit kleiner Sext, wird
nicht gefunden; hiermit soll ihr aber die Existenz nicht versagt
werden, obgleich als wahrscheinlich anzunehmen ist, dass die

---

1) Der Verf. wurde durch den Aberglauben der Indianer verhin-
dert, Beispiele der gebräuchlichsten Trauergesänge, die sehr wahrscheinlich in dieser Tonart gesungen werden, in seine Sammlung aufzunehmen.
Der seltene Gebrauch der kleinen Terz in den vorliegenden Melodien
darf nicht als maassgebend für die Indianergesänge überhaupt betrachtet
werden (vgl. XXXIII bis XLIII).

Phrygische (der schon angeführten Gründe wegen) unter den Tonarten mit Mollterz die beliebteste sei.

Nach Angabe der griechischen Theoretiker[1]) war es die Lydische, die Phrygische und die Dorische Tonart, welche sich am frühesten unter den Griechen herausbildeten; mit Ausnahme der letzteren stimmen diese ältesten Tonarten der Griechen mit denen der nordamerikanischen Indianer auffallend überein.

---

Im einleitenden Paragraphen wurde gesagt, die Indianermusik sei der wahre und höhere Ausdruck des Gefühls (»höhere« im Gegensatz zur trivialen Nachahmung der Natur). In der modernen Musik hängt die Wahl der Tonart, in welcher die Melodie eines Liedes sich bewegen soll, sowie das Zeitmaass und die Vortragsweise überhaupt wesentlich vom Charakter der Stimmung, welche durch die Musik znm Ausdruck gelangen soll, ab.

Ueber die Beziehung der Harmonien der Dur- und Molldreiklänge zum Gefühl hat sich **Moritz Hauptmann** ausführlich und feinfühlend ausgesprochen;[2]) der Gebrauch dieser Dreiklänge in rein melodischen Folgen, also als gebrochene Accorde, ist wohl denselben ästhetischen Grundsätzen unterworfen. Abgesehen also vom Zeitmaasse, in dem eine Melodie gesungen wird, sowie von den sonstigen Eigenthümlichkeiten der Vortragsweise des Sängers, würde man von diesem erwarten, dass er für solche Lieder, die eine fröhliche, spielende, oder muthige Stimmung verkünden oder erwecken sollen, eine Tonart, in welcher der Durcharakter vorherrschend ist, wählen würde; dass er dagegen für traurige, düstere oder weiche Gesänge die Molltonarten zu brauchen hätte. Im Grunde hat der Naturmensch dieselben Gefühle wie der Civilisirte, obgleich weder so complicirt, noch seiner einfachen Lebensweise wegen, in solcher

---

1) Paul, Absol. Harmonik der Griechen, S. 12—13.
2) Die Lehre von der Harmonik, Leipzig 1868. Eine Wiederholung seiner geistreichen, Jedermann zugänglichen Worte, wäre hier kaum am Platze.

Mannigfaltigkeit. Wird dies und auch das Obengesagte zuge-
geben, dass die Indianermusik der wahre und höhere Ausdruck
des menschlichen Gefühls ist, so wäre man zu dem Schluss berechtigt, dass der Indianer, um dieselben Gefühle wie der Civilisirte zum Ausdruck zu bringen, auch dieselbe Wahl der Tonarten treffen muss, dass seine Melodien somit sich weder ausschliesslich in Moll bewegen dürften, sondern eine dem Inhalt
der Lieder angemessene Abwechslung zeigen müssten. — In
folgenden Bemerkungen wird die Bezeichnung »Lydisch« resp.
»Hypophrygisch« durch die einfachere »Dur«, und »Phrygisch«
durch »Moll« ersetzt werden, wodurch der Charakter der Tonart mit hinreichender Deutlichkeit bezeichnet wird; zum besse-
ren Verständniss werden Tempo und Vortragsweise ebenfalls
angegeben.

I. Andante; Stimmung sanft, religiös, aber heiter —
*Dur*.

II. Allegretto; Danksagungslied, ehrfurchtsvoll —
*Moll*.

III. Rasch, wild, athemlos; Wolftanz — *Moll*.

IV. und V. Schnell; heitere Tänze — *Dur*.

VI. Andante con moto, spielend, heiter — *Dur*.

VII. und VIII. Allegro risoluto; muthige Kriegsgesänge
— *Dur*.

IX. Andante con moto; Gesang des entschlossenen
Kriegers.

X. Andante con moto, mezza voce; tiefe Ehrfurcht.

XI. Allegro; fröhlicher Lieblingstanz mehrerer Indianernationen — *Dur*.

XII. Andante con moto; Nachtgesang oder Ständchen —
*Dur*.

XIII. Sehr rasch; siegesgewiss, doch freundlich — *Dur*.

XIV. Rasch; mit halbgeschlossenem Mund, grausam —
*Moll*.

XV. Mässig schnell; Sturmlied, anfangs fröhlich, aber
mit mollartigem Schluss (kleine Septime) — *Dur*.

XVI. Mässig schnell; wehmüthiges Siegeslied (kleine Septime); wie

XVII. Mässig schnell; eine Art Gebet um den Schutz Gottes in der Schlacht — *Moll.*

XVIII. Allegretto; heiteres Liebeslied — *Dur.*

XIX und XX. Allegretto; Danksagungstänze, fröhlich.

XXI. Rasches, jubelndes Siegeslied — *Dur.*

XXII. Mässig schnell, Danksagungstanz der Weiber, fröhlich — *Dur.*

XXIII. Nicht schnell; Lied der Mutter zum abwesenden Sohn (überm. Quarte), klagend — *Dur.* [1]

XXIV. Nicht schnell; wehmüthiges Liebeslied, klagend — *Dur.* [1]

XXV und XXVI. Rasche, feurige Kriegslieder — *Dur.*

XXVII. Andante con moto; Kriegslied, den Verlust eines Häuptlings beklagend — *Dur.* [2]

XXVIII und XXIX. Allegro; fröhliche Tanzlieder — *Dur.*

XXX. Allegretto; Liebeslied — *Dur.*

XXXI. Allegro; Kriegslied — *Dur.*

XXXII. Lebhaftes, lustiges Tanzlied — *Dur.*

Es ist wohl kaum zu erwarten, dass diese Lieder, ihrer natürlichen, wilden Umgebung entrissen, hier denselben Eindruck machen sollten wie dort. Wie anders aber erscheint jene edle Alpenblume, das Edelweiss, in ihrer freien, luftigen Heimath, als wenn sie, unten im Thale, unter bunten Gartengewächsen ihr kümmerliches Dasein fristet! Freilich wird sie von Niemandem so hoch geschätzt, als von Dem, der sie selbst gepflückt hat!

---

## § 5. Melodische Folgen.

Jede Melodie hat eine zweifache Art der Bewegung; die rhythmische [3] und die intervallartige [4]. Ueber

---

1) In diesen Liedern kam der klagende Ton hauptsächlich durch eine passende Vortragsweise zum Ausdruck.

2) Ist mehr wie ein Tanzlied; in der Ausführungsweise war wenig Klagendes zu bemerken.

3) Recitative ausgenommen.

4) Monotone (wie X) ausgenommen.

die rhythmische Bewegungsart wird unter »Rhythmus« ausführlich gesprochen; vorliegender Paragraph hat sich daher nur mit der intervallartigen zu beschäftigen. Diese hat wiederum eine zweifache Art der Bewegung; erstens die schrittweise Bewegung und zweitens, die sprungweise Bewegung; welche beide, mit einander verbunden und abwechselnd und nur in den seltensten Fällen getrennt und selbständig auftretend, die melodischen Folgen bilden. Sollten nun diese letzteren bloss als zufällig, ohne irgend einen festen Anhaltepunkt oder geregelte Aufeinanderfolge erscheinen, so wären sie nur ein plan- und formloses Umherirren der Töne; wie aber bereits im vorhergehenden Paragraphen gezeigt worden, hat unter diesen Melodien eine jede eine feste Basis, einen Grundton, und zu diesem gesellt sich in jedem Beispiele die Quinte. Je bestimmter der Gegensatz zwischen Grundton und Quinte erscheint, desto deutlicher tritt der Character der Tonart hervor, wie durch das unmittelbare Aufeinanderfolgen dieser beiden Tonstufen, oder deren einfache Verbindung durch die Terz. In einigen Melodien (I, XIV und XXVIII) sind nur Grundton, Terz und Quinte, also die Glieder des tonischen Dreiklangs zu finden. In II zeigt sich ein höherer Grad der melodischen Entwickelung; hier fängt die Melodie mit der Quinte $e'$ an, schreitet durch die Mollterz $c'$ zum Grundton $a$ und, nach Wiederholung dieser Folge, zur Quinte $e$ hinab; diese jetzt als Basis benutzend geht die Melodie aus dem tonischen Accord zum Dominantenaccord $e$ $g$ $(a)$ $h$ über, dann nach $g$ zurück, und wieder zum Grundton $a$, (die kleine Septime wird hier sowohl auf- wie absteigend gebraucht); hierauf folgen Quinte $e$, Grundton $a$, kleine Septime $g$ $(=$ Dominantterz$)$, Grundton $a$, und nochmals die kleine Septime, alle stark, letztere wiederholt, betont; von diesem $g$ aus schreitet die Melodie durch die Secunde $h$ zur Quinte $e'$ hinauf, in welcher Folge der Dominantenaccord wieder zum Vorschein kommt; die schon angegebenen Folgen werden jetzt wiederholt, und die Melodie schliesst auf der Quinte mit Zuziehung des Grundtons. Aus diesem kurzen Ueberblick ergiebt sich nicht allein, dass Grundton und Quinte als besonders bevorzugte Momente zur Anwendung kommen, sondern auch, dass die auf diesen beiden Tonstufen basirenden Dreiklänge (als gebrochene Accorde *a c e′* resp. *e g h*) allein in der sprungweisen Bewegung angewendet werden, und dass durch die schrittweise Bewegung lediglich eine Verbindung dieser beiden Accorde, oder ein Uebergang vom einen zum andern, erzielt wird. — Folgende, den übrigen Melodien entnommene Beispiele der Melodieführung oder des Fortschreitens der Melodie von einer Tonstufe zur andern werden die Beziehung zwischen Grundton und Quinte verdeutlichen: die römische Zahl giebt die Nummer der betreffenden Melodie, der in runden Klammern eingefasste Buchstabe deren Grundton, und die arabische Zahl den Tact, in welchem das Beispiel gefunden wird, an.

Die Secunde, durch welche Bezeichnung stets die grosse gemeint wird, wendet sich: — 1. zum Grundton, entweder direct [XI (*c*) 3] oder durch die Terz[1] [IV (*g*)] oder durch die Quinte [XII (*c*) 10] oder durch die Septime (abwärts) [II (*a*) 5] oder durch die Quarte, zurück auf sich selbst, und sodann direct zum Grundton [VI (*g*) 7]; — 2. zur Terz durch die Quarte [XI (*c*) 11] oder durch die Quinte [XII (*c*) 21]; — 3. zur Quinte direct [II (*a*) 10] oder durch die Quarte [XIII (*d*) 10] oder durch die Terz [XXVI (*b*) 4].

----

1) D. h., die Secunde findet erst im Grundton einen augenblicklichen Ruhepunkt.

In diesen Beispielen, wo das Wesentliche in der Führung der Secunde zur bequemeren Uebersicht zusammengebracht worden ist, zeigt sie sich durch ihre Stellung in den verschiedenen melodischen Folgen auf's bestimmteste als Dominantquinte, d. h. als Glied des Dominanten- bez. Dominantseptimenaccords.

Die Quarte wendet sich: — 1. zum Grundton direct [IV (g) aufsteigend], [XIII (d) absteigend] oder durch die Secunde [III (a) 11] oder durch die Terz [III (a) Schluss] oder durch die Quinte [V (e) 18]; — 2. zur Terz direct [VIII (c) 7] oder durch die Quinte [III (a) 1]; — 3. zur Quinte direct [V (e) 14] oder durch die Terz [III (a) 6].

Eine unmittelbare Aufeinanderfolge von Quarte und Sext oder umgekehrt findet in keiner der vorliegenden Melodien statt, ebensowenig eine indirecte Verbindung dieser beiden Tonstufen (in dem Sinne, als wären sie Glieder eines und desselben Accords) [vergl. XVIII (g) 19]; deshalb kommt der Unterdominantdreiklang (als gebrochener Accord) gar nicht zur Anwendung; anstatt als Basis dieses Accords erscheint die Quarte in solchen Fällen, wo sie direct zum Grundton schreitet, eher als ein imperfecter, hastiger Uebergang vom Dominantseptimenaccord zum tonischen Accord, dies um so mehr, als in den meisten Fällen die ihr unmittelbar vorangehende Tonstufe entweder Quinte [XIII (d) 13] oder Secunde [XI (c) 36] ist.

Die Sext schreitet: — 1. zum Grundton direct [VII (c) 10] oder durch die Secunde [XXX (g) 4. v. Schluss; das einzige Beispiel]; — 2. zur Quinte direct [V (e) 2] oder durch die Secunde (aufsteigend) [XII (c) 6. v. Schluss, das einzige Beispiel]; — 3. zur Terz direct [XXII (c) 3, das einzige Beispiel], oder durch die Quinte [VIII (c) 9.]

Wie schon oben gesagt, erscheint in diesen Melodien das Verhältniss der Sext zur Quarte (also als Terz in einem möglichen Unterdominantenaccord), von wenig Bedeutung; man könnte zwar in verschiedenen Fällen eine Quarte als Unterdominante hinzudenken und so die Harmonie des Unterdominantdreiklangs der Melodie theoretisch unterschieben; die Thatsachen aber, dass dieser Dreiklang nicht ein Mal als gebrochener Accord vorkommt, und dass Quarte und Sext nicht ein Mal unmittelbar verbunden erscheinen, macht die Annahme, dass dem Indianer die Harmonie des Unterdominantdreiklangs wirklich vorschwebe, und dass er die Führung seiner Melodien gewissermassen darnach richte, zu einer sehr problematischen. Desto wichtiger ist die Stellung der Sext als Uebergang zwischen Grundton und Quinte (absteigend), in solchen Folgen wie Secunde, Grundton, Sext und Quinte, oder auch nur die drei letzten; in welchen Folgen die Sext als Dominantsecunde dasselbe Verhältniss zur Quinte hat, wie in ähnlichen

Folgen (Quinte, Quarte, Secunde und Grundton absteigend) die tonische Secunde zur Tonica.

Durch den häufigen Gebrauch der Sext als tonische Unterterz[1]) gewinnen mehrere Melodien einen weichen, mollartigen Character, welcher besonders da, wo sich die tonische Oberterz zu dieser Verbindung gesellt, hervortritt;

die bereits angeführten Beispiele haben die Abhängigkeit der Sext vom Grundton und Quinte so deutlich gezeigt, dass es kaum als gerechtfertigt erschiene, sie hier als Basis eines, vom Indianer anerkannten Accordes anzusehen; eher wäre der Grundton als der Anziehungspunkt zu betrachten, von welchem Terz und Sext, als Ober- resp. Unterterz gleich abhängig erscheinen.

Die Septime schreitet: — 1. zum Grundton direct [II (a) 4, 5], [V (e) 6] oder durch die Quinte [II (a) Schluss].

---

1) Dieser Begriff findet seine Begründung in solchen Beispielen wie VII (c) 10; VIII (c) 3; XII (e) 6. v. Schl.; XVIII (g) 13, u. s. w.

3

[XIV (a) 9] ; — 2. zur Quinte direct [VII (c) 15], [XIV (a) 12] oder durch die Secunde [II (a) 9] ;

in einem Beispiele [V (e) 6] hat sie keine ausgesprochene Verbindung mit den andern Gliedern des Dominantenaccords; sonst ist ihre Stellung als Dominantterz unverkennbar.

Aus dieser Untersuchung geht hervor, dass die Secunde ihre hauptsächliche Bedeutung als Dominantquinte hat; die Quarte erscheint in den meisten Fällen als Dominantseptime und die Septime als Dominantterz; dass diese drei Intervalle also ihre wesentliche Bestimmung, als Glieder des Dominanten- bez. Dominantseptimenaccords, von der Quinte, der Basis dieser Accorde, erhalten. Die Terz, als Glied des tonischen Accords, ist vom Grundton abhängig; die Quinte erscheint bald wie Dominante, wie die Basis eines Accords, — bald wie vom Grundton, als Quinte des tonischen Accords, abhängig. Die Stellung dieser Intervalle in den melodischen Folgen ist mithin eine solche, dass sie entweder im Grundton, als Basis eines gebrochenen Accords, ihre wesentliche Bestimmung finden, oder in der Quinte, wie in II bereits gezeigt worden. Dass diese beiden Accorde dem inneren Sinn des Indianers wirklich vorschweben, ist nach dem vorliegenden Material nicht mit Sicherheit zu entscheiden; dass Grundton und Quinte aber die eigentlichen Angelpunkte seiner Melodien sind, ist klar; die schwebende Stellung der Sext, bald vom Grundton, bald von der Quinte, angezogen und nirgends als bestimmtes Glied des Unterdominantenaccordes hervortretend, bekräftigt diese Annahme; die wenigen Unregelmässigkeiten in der Melodieführung liefern keine hinreichenden Gegenbeweise. Für die dominirende Stellung von Tonica und Quinte liefern die Schlüsse der Melodien den schlagendsten Beweis. Aus zweiunddreissig Melodien schliessen sechszehn auf dem Grundton und elf auf der Quinte, je eine auf der Terz und Sext, drei sind unvollständig [1].

## § 6. Rhythmus.

Die einfachste rhythmische Form entsteht aus einer Aufeinanderfolge von Schlägen, Tönen, oder sonstigen hörbaren Lauten, welche mit gleicher Stärke und in gleicher Zeitentfernung von einander erfolgen. Gesetzt nun, dass solche, sich stets gleichbleibende, Zeitabschnitte durch gleichmässige Schläge markirt und begrenzt werden, so darf nur dem Niederschlag eine bestimmt rhythmische Beschaffenheit zugedacht werden; denn, käme dem Heben der Hand, um weitere Schläge auszuführen, eine rhythmische Bedeutung zu, so würde dieses Heben der Hand als Aufschlag (Arsis) und der Niederschlag als Thesis erscheinen, wodurch das einfache Zeitmoment in ein zweifaches verwandelt wäre. Dieses erste rhythmische Moment, die einfache Ordnung in der Zeit, steht somit zwischen dem Ungeordneten und dem Tacte; unter dem Begriff »Tact« wird die regelmässige Wiederkehr eines Hauptaccents verstanden, und dieser setzt die Existenz eines Nebenaccents voraus; die einfachste Tactform besteht also aus einem Haupt- und einem Nebenaccent, ist somit ein Zweifaches, während das erste rhythmische Moment ein Einfaches ist.

---

1) Ueber den Schluss (clausula) schreibt Calvisius: »Diese Endigung geschieht hauptsächlich in den Endtönen des Intervalles Quinte, ganz besonders aber auf dem untersten Tone (d. h. also auf der Tonica), wo auch das vollständige Ende (finis) einer Melodie festgestellt wird, dann auch auf dem obersten Tone (d. h. also auf der Dominante).......
und in der Mitte, wo die Quinte in grosse und kleine Terz getheilt wird«,.... Wir würden einfach sagen, dass der Dreiklang die Töne für die Schlüsse liefere. [Paul, Absolute Harmonik der Griechen, S. 41, »Klarstellung der Tonarten des 16. Jahrh.«]

3*

Die Gesänge I bis incl. XXXII werden von gerade solchen monotonen Schlägen, wobei die Ausführenden nur auf das regelmässige Erfolgen der Niederschläge Rücksicht nehmen [1]), begleitet. Die Schläge werden entweder mit Ratteln, Stöcken, auf Pauken oder mit dem Fuss ausgeführt (in einigen Fällen, z. B. IV und V, mit den drei ersten zusammen): diese Art und Weise, den Rhythmus zu markiren, ist unter den Indianern weitverbreitet [2]), und scheint, soweit die Erfahrung des Verf. reicht, den Sängern fast zur zweiten Natur geworden zu sein, so dass sie oft nicht im Stande waren, ohne eine solche Begleitung ihre Lieder zu singen. Der Hauptzweck dieser lärmenden, monotonen rhythmischen Schläge scheint zu sein, die Ordnung unter tanzenden Massen zu erhalten; daher auch die Unzahl tactmarkirender Instrumente [vergl. »Instrumente«] und deren allgemeiner Gebrauch. Die Stimmen der geübtesten Sänger haben, bei solchen grösseren Tanzfesten, wo nur wenige singen, keine hinreichende Kraft, um durch das eintönige Getrampel der Tanzenden durchzudringen; in solchen Festen, in welchen die Tanzenden selbst singen, ist diese Begleitung ebenfalls unentbehrlich. — Bis jetzt war nur vom Markiren des Rhythmus die Rede; wie ist nun das Verhältniss zwischen diesem, und dem stimmlichen oder melodischen Accent? — Von diesem Verhältniss, auf der niedrigsten Stufe der Kunstentwickelung des Indianers, haben wir in dem, § 1 erwähnten Tanze der Dogrib-Indianer ein ungefähres Bild; will man einen Anfang zur rhythmischen Evolution suchen, so ist es wohl kaum nothwendig, in die Kunstgeschichte des Indianers weiter zurückzugreifen; dieser rohe Tanz hat einen unverkennbar uranfänglichen Character. Erstens: hier erscheint die rhythmische Bewegung, überall ein Hauptmoment in den geselligen Tänzen der Indianer, der eigentliche Zweck der ganzen Aufführung zu sein, dem die Worte und Melodie [?] des Gesangs gänzlich untergeordnet sind; zweitens: der Rhyth-

---

[1]) Die einzige Ausnahme wird unten erwähnt.

[2]) Nach dem Character der Instrumente und Tänze zu beurtheilen, allgemein.

mus ist nicht tactartig, sondern monoton; drittens: es
wird kein tactmarkirendes Instrument gebraucht. — Weil aber
die Art und Weise, den Rhythmus zu markiren, auch in den
vorliegenden, melodisch verhältnissmässig hochentwickelten
Gesängen, denselben monotonen Character trägt, so ist der
Fortschritt in der Entwickelung der Tactform aus der Monotonie offenbar in der Melodie zu suchen [1]. Erscheint also
der Gesang anfangs wie an den monotonen rhythmischen Schlägen festgebunden, so wäre der nächste Schritt in der rhythmischen Evolution, der Melodie etwas mehr Freiheit der Bewegung zu verschaffen, indem die gesungenen Töne, anstatt
immer mit gleichem Accent und zu gleicher Zeit mit den Schlägen einzutreffen, auch neben oder zwischen diesen einfielen
oder einen individuellen Accent erhielten; einen solchen Grad
der Entwickelung zeigt das Lied Nr. X [2] (ein uralter, gottes-
dienstlicher Gesang).

Yu - ö   wi hi   yu wi hi - ö   yu - ö   wi hi

Dieses Lied wurde von Männern allein gesungen, die um
zwei, mitten im Tanzsaale aufgestellte Holzbänke herumtrab-
ten; der Haupt- (»individuelle«) accent ist mit (<) angezeigt;
bei jedem Schritte in ihrer ungraziösen, lockeren Bewegung
wurde ein etwas schwächerer Accent ausgestossen (genau
wie im Dogrib Tanze). Nr. IV liefert ein Beispiel der auf die
Spitze getriebenen Unregelmässigkeit in der melodischen Accentuation.

---

1) Nachstehendes trägt, was den rhythmischen Entwicke-
lungsgang betrifft, selbstverständlich einen nur hypothetischen Character; für die Richtigkeit der Thatsachen bürgt des Verf. eigene
Erfahrung.

2) Die Schläge (bez. die Tritte der Tanzenden) werden auf der
über das Liniensystem hinzugefügten Linie notirt; wie in den übrigen
Beispielen ist ein Schlag einer Viertelnote (♩) gleich (im geraden Tact);
im ungeraden einer Viertelnote mit Punkt (♩.).

[Weitere Beispiele der primitivsten Gesänge findet man XXXIX]. Hier ist keine bloss vorübergehende, gleich ausgeglichene Accentverschiebung, wie sie in sonst regelmässigen, tactartigen Melodien oft vorkommt; es wird vielmehr die Unregelmässigkeit zur Regel. Dieser wild dahinstürmenden Melodie ist der Begriff »Tact« nicht anzupassen; sie sucht sich von der beschwerlichen Monotonie der rhythmischen Begleitung durch seltsame Sprünge und gewaltsames Hin- und Herzerren des Accents loszuwinden, wird aber trotzdem von der unbezwinglichen rhythmischen Flut hingerissen. [1]

Das Gleichgewicht zwischen Rhythmus und Melodie wird erst durch die Ausbildung der Tactform hergestellt. Dies kann auf zweierlei Weise geschehen; erstens, kann der melodische Hauptaccent mit j e d e m Schlag zusammenfallen, die Melodie

---

1) Viele dieser Melodien machen factisch den Eindruck, als würden sie vom Rhythmus getragen und fortgeschleppt.

aber, anstatt der einfachen rhythmischen Bewegung der
Schläge, eine zwei-, drei- oder vierfache Bewegung erhalten, sich also (wenn ein Schlag gleich einer Viertelnote,
bez. einer Viertelnote mit Punkt, gesetzt wird) im $^2/_8$, $^3/_8$, oder
$^4/_{16}$ Tact bewegen; — zweitens, kann der melodische Hauptaccent, anstatt mit jedem Schlage, mit jedem zweiten,
dritten, oder vierten Schlag zusammentreffen, woraus der
$^2/_4$, $^3/_4$, oder $^4/_4$ Tact entsteht. Hiermit hätten wir sechs tact-
artige rhythmische Bewegungsarten gewonnen; von allen die-
sen sind in den vorliegenden Melodien Beispiele zu finden [IX
ist zwar nicht vollständig, lässt sich aber, soweit hier angegeben, ebenso richtig im $^3/_4$ wie im $^2/_8$ Tact schreiben]. — Beim
Bestimmen des Tactmaasses, in dem eine Melodie notirt werden
soll, sucht der Zuhörer sich so viel wie möglich vom Gefühl
der Eintönigkeit, welches durch das monotone Erfolgen der
Schläge erzeugt wird, zu befreien, und sich, so gut es geht,
nach dem melodischen Accent zu richten; bei diesem Ver-
such aber wird er bald gewahr, dass in manchen Fällen der
innerliche Widerstreit zwischen Rhythmus und Melodie nicht
ganz geschlichtet ist, und dass rhythmische Unregelmässigkeiten
häufig wiederkehren, wie in den Liedern I und II. Um ihre
rhythmischen Eigenthümlichkeiten verständlich zu machen,
folgt eine kurze Beschreibung des Erntefesttanzes der Irokesen.

Das »Tanzhaus«, ein ca. 50 Fuss langes, 30 Fuss breites
Brettergebäude, hat ein einziges, grosses Zimmer, den »Tanz-
saal«, um dessen Wände zwei Reihen Sitzplätze für Zuschauer
aufgeschlagen sind; mitten im Saale stehen zwei längliche,
niedrige Holzbänke; den übrigen Raum nehmen die Tanzenden in Anspruch. Der Hauptsänger, der zu gleicher Zeit als
Dirigent der ganzen Aufführung fungirt, sitzt rittlings auf der
einen Holzbank; ihm gegenüber, auf derselben Bank, sitzt ein
zweiter Sänger, in einer solchen Entfernung, dass die grossen
Ratteln, von welchen jeder Sänger eine zum Markiren des
Rhythmus in der Hand hält, sich nicht aneinander stossen.
Die tanzlustigen jungen Krieger gehen mit kurzen, langsamen
Schritten um die beiden Sänger im Kreise herum. Der Diri-
gent fängt nun mit seiner in beiden Händen gehaltenen Rattel

auf die Holzbank zu klopfen an und wird vom anderen Sänger auf's genaueste begleitet; anfangs fallen die Schläge langsam und schwach, nehmen aber immer an Schnelligkeit und Heftigkeit zu, bis das richtige Zeitmaass erreicht wird; (dies wird vor fast jedem Liede des Erntefests wiederholt, als wollten sich die Sänger zusammennehmen, und die Lieder ins Gedächtniss zurückrufen); sodann ruft der Dirigent den Kriegern zu: »Wollt Ihr anfangen?«; diese antworten, wie ein Mann, mit einem lauten, zustimmenden Ausruf, und das Lied beginnt, zuerst von einfachen Schlägen, bald aber von Doppelschlägen, die mit einer solchen Geschwindigkeit ausgeführt werden, dass jeder fast wie ein einziger Schlag erscheint, begleitet. Bei der Wiederholung der Melodie werden die einfachen Schläge wieder gebraucht, doch so, dass nur einer um den andern die Holzbank trifft, während für jeden zweiten Schlag die Rattel nur nach unten geschwenkt wird, ungefähr wie ein Capellmeister, wenn er ein Musikstück im 2/4 Tact dirigirt, den Tactstock bewegt. (Der einfache Schlag = ♩; der Doppelschlag ♩: das Schwenken der Rattel, ohne einen Schlag auszuführen = o).

Ka yoñ a hi a de ni ta-a ha wi noñ he he a hän

hän soñ guai hua yo ni he he a hän hän ka yon hi a

de he ha e hän hän ka yoñ a hi a de · ni ta-a ha wi

noñ he he a hăñ hăñ soñ gua-i hua yo ni he he a hăñ

hăñ ka yoñ hi ya de he he a hăñ hăñ ho! a ho!

Yo soñ gua we ni yo hăñ-ăñ yo ho ho ho hăñ-ăñ yo

hăñ-ăñ! yo hăñ-ăñ hăñ-ăñ soñ gua we ni yo

hăñ-ăñ yo ho ho ho hăñ-ăñ yo hăñ-ăñ yo hăñ-ăñ

hăñ-ăñ yo son gua we ni yo hăñ-ăñ yo ho ho ho

hăñ-ăñ yo hăñ-ăñ! yo hăñ-ăñ hăñ-ăñ hăñ yo! h'yo!

Die Bewegungen der Füsse der Tanzenden stimmen auf's genaueste (auch in ihrer Gleichmässigkeit, da nicht der Tact,

sondern nur der Rhythmus, markirt wird) mit dem Character der Schläge überein. Zu Anfang eines jeden Liedes balanciren sich die Tänzer, so lange die einfachen Schläge fallen, leicht von einem Fusse zum andern; sobald die Doppelschläge anfangen, werden mit einem Fusse nach dem andern ebenfalls Doppelschläge mit heftigem Stampfen und einer förmlichen Wuth ausgeführt; der Lärm wird von kleinen, um das Knie gebundenen Schellen vermehrt und steigert sich bei Tänzen in tempo prestissimo zu einem unbeschreiblichen Getöse. — In I ist eine starke Neigung zum $^2/_4$ Tact bemerkbar ohne eine consequente Durchführung; in II ist dieselbe Tactform fast ganz regelmässig ausgebildet: man hat nur das bei der ersten Wiederholung von »Soñ gua« während zwei Schläge gehaltene $h$ als eine verlängerte Viertelnote $\left( \right)$ zu schreiben, um diese Melodie als vollkommen geordnet erscheinen zu lassen; die Schreibweise $h =$ ist jedoch richtiger, da die Zeitdauer dieser Note der für zwei Schläge in Anspruch genommenen Zeit genau entspricht. (Aehnliche Fälle sind in V und XI zu finden).

Um auf die schon erwähnten Tactarten ($^2/_8$, $^3/_8$, $^4/_{16}$, $^2/_4$, $^3/_4$ und $^4/_4$) zurückzukommen, ist zunächst die Thatsache hervorzuheben: dass, aus zweiunddreissig Melodien, nur fünf im ungeraden Tact, dagegen vierundzwanzig im geraden Tacte sich bewegen (I, IV und X werden nicht als tactförmig betrachtet), und dass von diesen letzteren nur zwei im $^4/_4$ Tact, während zweiundzwanzig im $^2/_8$ oder $^2/_4$ Tacte sind. Von den fünfzehn Melodien im $^2/_4$ Tact werden dreizehn von Tänzen, welche eine abwechselnde Thätigkeit der beiden Füsse nöthig machen, begleitet. Da nun die meisten Gesänge, besonders unter den weniger entwickelten Indianervölkern, von Tänzen begleitet werden, so ist es durchaus nicht unwahrscheinlich, dass der $^2/_4$ Tact gerade in dieser abwechselnden Thätigkeit der Füsse seinen Ursprung hatte, und dass dieser mit dem $^2/_8$ Tact die ersten, ursprünglichen Tactformen waren. [1]

---

1) Unter den Chippewas sollen die gebräuchlichsten Tactformen $^2/_4$

Aus den schon angegebenen Tactformen bilden sich in mehreren Melodien zusammengesetzte Tacte; in VI, welche sich in drei gleiche Abschnitte oder rhythmische Reihen zertheilen lässt, jede Reihe zu vier Tacten; VII, wo jede Reihe vier Tacte enthält, und von den übrigen scharf ¦abgesondert ist; IX enthält fünf Reihen zu drei Tacten; XVII hat neun solche Reihen; XXVII enthält vier Reihen; XXVIII sechs, und XXXI acht Reihen zu zwei Tacten; XXX hat vier Reihen zu vier Tacten.

Im XV. Liede fällt der melodische Ictus jedesmal mit dem Wortaccent zusammen; in den anderen dakota und ebenso in den alten gottesdienstlichen Liedern (wie I, II, III, IV, V, X, XIX, XX, XXXII) ist dies nicht der Fall; Beispiele wie X und besonders IV zeigen, dass der Accent auf jede Weise herumgezerrt werden kann. Das Verhältniss des Wortaccents zum melodisch-rhythmischen und die Ursachen der verschiedenen Formen der Accentverschiebung, würden ein sehr interessantes Capitel bilden; eine solche Untersuchung kann aber nur dann mit wahrem Erfolg unternommen werden, wenn der Forscher eine umfassende Kenntniss der Indianersprachen oder einen ausgezeichneten Dolmetscher hat; dem Verf. steht keins von beiden zur Verfügung. — In den Reden der Irokesen, wenn dieselben einen officiellen Character haben, wird jede Periode mit einem tiefen, rauhen Kehllaut begonnen, worauf die höhere

---

und $^4/_4$ sein (brfl. Mitth. a. d. Verf. vom Rev. I. Baird), unter den Pueblo Indianern $^2/_4$, $^3/_4$, $^4/_4$ (br. M. v. Rev. T. F. Ealy), unter den Dakotas, Gesänge grösstentheils $^2/_4$, Flötenmusik $^3/_4$ (br. M. v. Rev. A. L. Riggs), unter den Micmacs $^2/_4$, $^4/_4$, $^3/_4$ (br. M. v. R. P. Eugène Vetromile), unter den Twanas sind aus 24 Gesängen 20 im geraden Tact (vergl. XXXIX). — In einer Sammlung von Liedern der Neger in den ehemaligen Sclavenstaaten sind, aus 136 Melodien, nur 6 im $^3/_4$ Tact, dagegen 83 im $^2/_4$, 45 im $^4/_4$, und 2 im $^6/_8$ Tact. Diese Melodien sind nicht, wie es in anderen Sammlungen der Fall ist, englischen Versen angepasst worden, sondern in ihrer orginellen, eigenthümlichen Gestalt wiedergegeben. (W$^m$ F. Allen, Slave Songs of the U. S., New York, 1867). Die Tänze der Neger sind bekanntlich mehr wegen des genauen Rhythmus, als wegen ihrer Grazie, bemerkenswerth. — Unter den Griechen waren in der vorhomerischen Zeit die zwei- und dreitheiligen Tactmaasse vorhanden.

Octave folgt, mit der grössten Heftigkeit ausgestossen: bis zum
Anfange der nächsten Periode bewegt sich die Rede, halbge-
sprochen, halbgesungen, in diesem Octavton und dessen Secunde also:

die Secunde scheint immer den Wortaccent, den »Hochton«.
zu tragen. In den Liedern fällt der melodische Accent stets
mit einem Schlag bez. Fusstritt zusammen, und in einigen der
älteren Gesänge (wie III und IV) scheinbar ohne Rücksicht auf
den prosodischen Accent; jedenfalls wurde anfänglich
mehr Gewicht auf die rhythmische Beschaffenheit der Melodien
(als Begleitung zu Tänzen), als auf das genaue Einhalten des
Silbenmaasses, oder auf den prosodischen Accent gelegt.

---

## § 7. Recitativ.

Die Frage, ob die Musik der Indianer zuerst die bestimmte oder rhythmische Form oder die unbe-
stimmte Gestalt des Recitativs hatte, ist von entschiedenem
Interesse. Wenn unter »Recitativ« solche uranfängliche, halb-
unbewusste Versuche wie das Aufjauchzen der Freude, das
jämmerliche Klagen der Trauer oder des körperlichen Schmerzes, oder das Nachahmen der Vögel und anderer Naturlaute
verstanden werden, so wäre das Recitativ ohne viel Bedenken
als die ältere Form der Musik anzunehmen. Ist aber von der
Ausübung einer Kunst, sei sie in einem noch so rohen
Zustande, die Rede, so erscheint das Recitativ in einem ganz
andern Lichte. Westphal[1]) entscheidet sich ohne weiteres für
das erstere, wenn er schreibt: »Das Rhythmische und Sym-
metrische in der Kunst ist älter und natürlicher als das Un-
rhythmische und Unsymmetrische«, und sich auf die Behauptung stützt, dem menschlichen Geiste sei der Sinn für abstracte

---

1) Elemente des musikalischen Rhythmus, Jena 1872, § 11.

Ordnung und Gleichmässigkeit immanent. — Als Abstraction würde die Behauptung ebenso gerechtfertigt erscheinen: das Recitativ entspringt, als reine Herzensergiessung, aus dem angebornen musikalischen Triebe und hat nicht nöthig die streng rhythmische Form anzunehmen, um als Kunst anerkannt zu werden [Westphal sagt (§ 10) »Der Rhythmus ist etwas was dem Rhythmizomenon, dem Bewegungsstoffe der musischen Künste, keineswegs nothwendig ist«]; der Natur der Sache gemäss von einer Person allein ausgeführt, steht er in innigster Verbindung mit, und auf der nächsten Stufe der Entwickelung über oben erwähnten »Versuchen«, wäre somit in der musikalischen Evolution als die ältere Form (im Gegensatz zur rhythmischen) zu betrachten.

Ueber diese Frage in Bezug auf die Musik der Indianer ist folgendes zu bemerken:

1. Der Zweck des weitaus grössten Theiles der Gesänge der wilden Indianer überhaupt, besonders aber unter den weniger entwickelten, ist das Zusammenwirken, und dieses erscheint stets als ein geordnetes oder rhythmisches. [Die Senecas z. B., die es nicht einmal soweit gebracht haben, Liebeslieder zu componiren, haben gar keine Gesänge, welche nicht zum Zusammensingen bestimmt wären, aufzuweisen; selbst Trauergesänge werden von mehreren Frauen zusammen gesungen. Ihre Lieder haben alle ohne Ausnahme eine rhythmische Form. Diejenigen Gesänge, welche von den Senecas selbst als die ältesten bezeichnet werden, sind die religiösen Tanzlieder].

2. Von solchen rhythmischen Gesängen ist eine ununterbrochene, consequente Reihenfolge aufzuweisen, vom rohesten Anfange bis zum nahezu vollendet metrischen Gesang [vergl. »Poesie« und »Rhythmus«].

3. Das Recitativ kann, seiner unregelmässigen, der Willkür des Sängers überlassenen Gestalt wegen, nur von einem Sänger gesungen werden; in den Gesängen aber, die von einer Person ausgeführt werden, hat die Melodie, in den einfacheren Beispielen, eine rhythmische Bewegung. [Vergl. XXXV; XXXIX; XLII; XLIII; »Webino« Gesänge 1 und 2 (unter

»Schriftzeichen«); über die cabbalistischen Gesänge der Zau-
berärzte unter den Dakotas schreibt Herr Prof. T. W. Chittenden (Appleton, Wis.) dem Verf., dass sie von der Rattel oder
Pauke begleitet werden (also rhythmisch); Catlin (Letters
and Notes, p. 370) sagt, dass der Dakota zu solchen Liedern
die er für sich allein in seiner Hütte singt, eine sanfte Pauken-
begleitung braucht. In einem Danksagungstanz der Senecas
sang der Führer zuerst einige Noten, die für sich rhythmisch
gehalten waren, obgleich sie mit dem Rhythmus des Tanzes
gar keinen Zusammenhang hatten, und wurde vom Chor auf
ƒ' (die Tonica seiner Melodie) beantwortet:

Ho hi ho hu, ho hi ho hu

hăn! hăn!

u. s. w., mit wenig Abwechselung].

4. Dieselben Schriftsteller, welche den rhythmischen Character der Indianergesänge mit Nachdruck betonen, sagen
nichts von einem Recitativ, bezeichnen vielmehr in solchen
Fällen, wo diese Gesangsform zu erwarten wäre, die Gesänge
ausdrücklich als rhythmische, z. B. wenn ein Krieger seine
Heldenthaten den andern vorsingt (Loskiel, S. 134); Powers,
Contributions to Amer. Ethnology, vol. III; ch. II (auch S.
235—7) sagt ausdrücklich, dass die Improvisationen der [Cali-
fornia-] Indianer streng rhythmisch sind.

5. Solche Improvisationen, in welchen diese Vortragsweise (das Recitativ) vorkommen dürfte, haben einen Fluss
der Worte und eine Deutlichkeit des Ausdrucks, welche mit
dem Begriff eines primitiven Gesangs durchaus unvereinbar
sind. [In Todesgesängen (vergl. Domenech, Seven Years'
Residence in the Great Deserts of N. Am., London, 1860,
p. 162); in Liebesliedern (ibid., p. 148); in improvisirten
Liedern über gute oder schlechte Nachrichten oder andere
Themata (vergl. H. H. Bancroft, vol. I, p. 738; — Rev.

M. Eells, in Amer. Antiquarian, April, Mai und Juni 1879,
p. 250)].

Das mangelhafte Material berechtigt keine endgültige Ent-
scheidung dieser Frage; die oben angeführten Thatsachen aber
deuten darauf hin, dass Westphal's S c h l u s s, in Bezug auf
die Gesänge der Indianer, ein richtiger ist, obgleich der von
ihm angegebene G r u n d angefochten werden kann. Was dem
Verf. als »keineswegs nothwendig« erscheint, ist: diese Frage
wie eine Abstraction zu behandeln, und sie von vornherein in
das Schattenreich der angebornen oder »immanenten« Ideen zu
verbannen, zumal wenn das Concrete und sogar leicht Fass-
liche, der Z w e c k, als eine hinreichende Ursache für die
rhythmische Bewegung erscheint. Das alltägliche Leben bietet
uns zahlreiche Beispiele der Nothwendigkeit des geordneten
Zusammenwirkens; zwei Personen, die zusammen durch die
Stadt gehen, müssen gleichen Schritt halten, damit sie sich
nicht gegenseitig stossen; jeder Feldwebel weiss, dass das
rhythmische Gefühl manchem seiner Recruten durchaus kein
angebornes ist; im Gegentheil erlernen diese das geordnete
Marschiren nur nach oft wiederholten Versuchen, und den un-
liebsamsten Erfahrungen. Wie kommt es aber, dass unter den
Indianern a l l e ein fest rhythmisches Gefühl haben? Erstens,
weil sie von der frühesten Kindheit auf diese Tänze ange-
sehen und mitgemacht haben; zweitens, weil das Bestreben,
der Führer der Reigen, der gewandeste und graziöseste Vor-
tänzer zu werden, durch den eigenen Ehrgeiz und das Beispiel
der angesehensten Rathgeber und Krieger unter diesen wilden
Völkern, stets erneuert und gestärkt wird. Die Monotonie der
einfachsten Form des Rhythmus, welche Prof. Westphal so un-
erträglich findet, giebt dem Wilden, wie schon gezeigt worden,
den nöthigen Anhaltepunkt für seine Aufführungen; die geordnete, i. e. rhythmische Bewegung ist die natürliche und
zwingende Bedingung, unter welcher diese Aufführungen stattfinden können, um angenehm zu sein; dass der Rhythmus
(selbst »der allerelementarsten Art«) dem menschlichen Geiste
a n g e n e h m und in den Tänzen der Wilden n ö t h i g erscheint,
ist entschieden kein Grund für die Behauptung, dass er »dem

menschlichen Geiste immanent« ist. Prof. Westphal meint zwar : »wir dürfen ungescheut die Behauptung aufstellen, dass der hier [§ 13] skizzirte erste Anfang der Poesie [die lyrische Gattung] zugleich der erste Anfang der Musik war«. Er lässt also die Musik erst dann anfangen, als die metrische Form der lyrischen Poesie vollendet war! und nennt diese Form »die rhythmische«, ohne wie es scheint zu bedenken, dass der Rhythmus den Stoff für die metrischen Formen liefert, und dass er diese Formen sehr leicht entbehren kann.

---

## § 8. Schriftzeichen.

Es ist nicht wahrscheinlich, dass die am Schlusse beige-gebenen Schriftzeichen eine directe Beziehung zu den Tönen der Melodien haben. Schoolcraft, aus dessen umfangreichem Werk [1] dieselben entnommen, spricht ihnen zwar einen solchen Character nicht rund ab; er findet aber, dass sie in Bezug auf die Worte der Gesänge keinen phonetischen, sondern einen mnemonischen Character haben, — dass die Zeichen also nur dazu bestimmt sind, den Gegenstand der Lieder ins Ge-dächtniss zurückzurufen. — Es ist nicht anzunehmen, dass diese Indianer, welchen es nicht eingefallen war, die einfache-ren Consonanten und Vocale in ihrer Schrift wiederzugeben, eine Notenschrift, welche die subtilen und wechselvollen Töne der Melodien festhalten sollte, erfinden könnten. Die Sänger suchen vielmehr ihr Gedächtniss derart zu stärken, dass sie mitten im geräuschvollsten Tanze die Geistesgegenwart nicht verlieren, sondern ihre Lieder ohne irgend welche mechanische Hülfe und oft sogar in einer bestimmten Ordnung absingen können. A-ō-doñ-wĕ versicherte, er singe die neunund-achtzig Lieder für's Erntefest immer in derselben Ordnung der Reihe nach, ohne sich lange besinnen zu müssen. Der

---

1) Archives of Aborginal Knowledge, Phila, 6 Bde Fo; vol. I, Plate 52, und pp. 366 und 373.

R. P. Eugène Vetromile, [1]) welcher der Schrift der Micmas und der verwandten Nationen seine besondere Aufmerksamkeit gewidmet hat, sagt ausdrücklich, dass diese Indianer jeden Gedanken, auch mit den verschiedensten Modificationen vermittelst ihrer Hieroglyphen ausdrücken könnten; dennoch hatten sie keine Notenschrift noch irgend ein Zeichen, welches Bezug auf Töne hatte. [2]) Rafinesque, [3]) der Uebersetzer der unter den Wapahani oder White River Indianern gefundenen »Wallam-Olum« (»gemalten Urkunden«), findet, dass dieselben dazu bestimmt waren, die Worte dieser historischen Gesänge auf mnemonische Weise zu erhalten, und sagt weiter: »Das Ganze ist bloss ein Verzeichniss ihrer Häuptlinge mit einigen hervorragenden Thaten, steht jedoch nicht hinter ähnlichen Documenten der Mexikaner.« [?]

Die sechs beigegebenen Symbole sind die ersten aus dreissig, welche auf einer Tafel von Birkenrinde gezeichnet waren; eine solche Tafel wird für gewöhnlich »Musik-Brett« genannt, weil von ihr die Gesänge abgesungen werden. Diese Symbole werden in gewissen Orgien eines weitverbreiteten Indianervereins, »Webino« [4]) genannt, gebraucht; auf diesem »Brett« waren sie in vier horizontalen Linien arrangirt; man fing in der unteren Ecke rechter Hand an, und las nach links.

»Fig. 1 ist der einleitende Gesang und zeigt die Abbildung einer für den nächtlichen Tanz eingerichteten Indianerhütte, die mit sieben Kreuzen, welche sieben Leichen vorstellen, und mit einem magischen Knochen und mit Federn gekrönt ist. Man bildet sich ein, die Hütte könne sich bewegen und herumkriechen. Derjenige, in dessen Hütte die übrigen Mitglieder des Vereins sich versammelt haben, singt allein:

---

1) Siehe dessen Werk »The Abnakis and their History«, New York, 1866, ch. VI.

2) Brfl. Mitth. a. d. Verf., vom 10 December 1880.

3) The Amer. Nations, vol. I, ch. V. — Vergl. »Poesie«.

4) Eine Bezeichnung für gewisse mitternächtige Orgien und beziehungsweise für die in solche Mysterien Eingeweihten, die eine besondere magische Kraft ausüben sollen. Eine freie Uebersetzung des Worts wäre »Männer des Tagesanbruchs«. [Schoolcraft.]

4

We bi no          (Webino)
Pi mo de          (er kriecht)
Ni wi gi wam      (meine Hütte) [D. C.]
    Hai ō he
    Nhu i we
    Nhu i we
    He! he! hu! hu! hu!
(Meine Hütte kriecht herum durch des Webino Gewalt.)

Fig. 2. Ein Indianer hält in der Hand eine Schlange; diese soll unter der Erde durch Zauberkraft gefangen worden sein, und wird als ein Triumph der Gewandtheit gezeigt.

    A nō
    Muk kum mig
    In doan
    Di nōn
    Nō muk
    Kum mig
    Hai ō he u. s. w.
(Unter der Erde habe ich sie genommen.)

Der zwischen 2. und 3. stehende Strich zeigt eine Pause an; von hier an singen alle zusammen und der Tanz beginnt, von den gewöhnlichen Instrumenten [Pauke und Ratteln] begleitet.

Fig. 3. Ein sitzender mit Federn gekrönter Indianer hält in der ausgestreckten Hand einen Paukenschlägel.

    Gai e nīn (G a i - e = auch)
    Ni we bi no
    Hai! e! i! [D. C.] (cabbalistisch.)
      (Auch ich bin ein Webino.)

Fig. 4. Ein auf dem halben Himmelsgewölbe tanzender Geist; die Hörner sollen entweder einen Geist oder einen von Geisterkraft durchdrungenen Webino bezeichnen.

    We bi no
    Nō ni mi ō [D. C.]
    Hai! e! i! u. s. w. (cabbal.)
(Ich heisse die Webinos tanzen.)

Fig. 5. Ein magischer Knochen mit Federn geschmückt; ein Symbol der Kraft sich durch die Luft, wie mit Flügeln, zu bewegen.

> Ki jig
> I mi
> In gi
> Ne osh
> Shi an
> Hai! e! i! u. s. w. (cabbal.)

(Den Himmel! den Himmel durchschwebe ich!)

Fig. 6. Eine grosse Schlange, »gitchy kinebik«, die stets, wie in diesem Falle, mit Hörnern gezeichnet wird. Sie ist das Sinnbild des Lebens.

> Mon i do
> Wi ōn
> E ko
> We bi no
> Nuk ke yōn.
> Hi! e! u. s. w.

(Ich bin ein Webino Geist; dies ist mein Werk.«)

---

## § 9. Instrumente.

**a. Schlaginstrumente.** — Diese finden in ihren verschiedenen Formen die weiteste Verbreitung und fehlen wohl keiner Indianernation gänzlich, doch nur in Mexiko, Centralamerika und den spanischen Inseln hatten sie eine bestimmte, mit der menschlichen Stimme oder anderen Instrumenten harmonirende Tonhöhe. Das vollkommenste Instrument dieser Gattung war:

Der Huehuetl[1] [huehuitl, vevtl[2] tlapanhuehuetl[3] ], eine in Mexiko und Centralamerika gebräuchliche Art Pauke.

---

1) Clavigero, Buch VII, Abschn. XLIV [mit Abbildung]; Torquemada, lib. XIV, cap. XI.

2) H. H. Bancroft, vol. III, pp. 62—63.

3) Brasseur, Grammaire de la langue Quiché, S. 10.

4 *

Der Huehuetl bestand aus einem cylindrischen, ausgehöhlten
Baumstamm oder Holzklotz, der auswendig geschnitzt und
bemalt, drei bis vier Fuss hoch, und so stark wie ein Mann
war, und aufrecht auf einem Dreifuss stand; das obere Ende
war mit Leder oder Pergament überzogen, welches, je nachdem der Ton höher oder tiefer sein sollte, mehr oder weniger
straff gezogen werden konnte. Er wurde mit den Fingern
geschlagen, wozu grosse Geschicklichkeit gehörte. Dieses
Instrument wurde vielfach mit dem Teponaztli zusammen gespielt, und wenn wir den alten spanischen Geschichtsschrei-
bern Glauben schenken können, in vollem harmonischen Ein-
klang mit demselben [vergl. »Teponaztli«]. Torquemada giebt
an, dass der Ton des Huehuetl vom Rande bis zur Mitte
des Trommelfells um eine Quinte wechselte [hace su diapente,
buchstäblich: »macht seine Quinte«], dass das Instrument »seines Tonwechsels und seiner Töne wegen« [por sus puntos, y
tonos] gespielt wurde, und dass die Töne mit den Gesängen
gestimmt bald höher, bald tiefer wurden. — Diese Begleitung scheint demnach ein harmonirender Bass gewesen zu sein.

Der Teponaztli [teponaztle, tepunaztli] (nach Brasseur[1]) vom Wort teponovoz in der Quiché-Sprache abge-
leitet, dasselbe Instrument wie der Tun) wird noch heute von
den Eingebornen in Mexiko und Centralamerika gebraucht.[2]
Er wurde stets aus hartem, oft sehr schön geschnitztem Holz
gefertigt; der zwei bis fünf Fuss[3] lange Holzblock, dessen
Seiten in seiner einfachsten Gestalt die runde Form des Baum-
stammes behielten,[4] in der kunstvolleren aber fast ins Geviert
bearbeitet wurden, wurde von unten ausgehöhlt, jedoch so,
dass die beiden Enden noch drei bis vier Zoll dick blieben;
oben in der Mitte machte man drei Einschnitte,[5] zwei der

---

1) Grammaire de la langue Quiché (Ballet-drame de Rabinal-Achi).
2) Ibid., (Essai, p. 10).
3) Clavigero, wie oben (mit Abb.).
4) Oviedo, parte I, lib. V, cap. I.
5) Ibid.; Torquemada, lib. XIV, cap. XI; Nebel, Voyage pittoresque,
Paris, 1836 (mit Abbildungen); dagegen geben Brasseur (Quatre
lettres, 2me L., § 7, Anmerk.) und Clavigero an, dass nur zwei parallel

Länge des Blocks nach, den dritten zwischen diesen, die drei also in der Form des Buchstaben ⊥. Die beiden auf diese Weise hergestellten Zungen, welche einen Durchmesser von einigen Linien hatten, liessen von den Schlägeln berührt zwei verschiedene Töne vernehmen, deren Intervallenverhältniss in verschiedenen Instrumenten die Terz, Quarte, Quinte, Sext oder Octave war.[1]) Der Ton des Teponaztli war sehr stark und oft wohlklingend;[2]) man konnte ihn bisweilen in der Entfernung einer Meile hören. In der Musik zum Ballet-Drama »Rabinal-Achi« scheint der Tun durchaus nicht mit den beiden Trompeten zu harmoniren; im Avant-propos zur Grammatik aber sagt Brasseur ausdrücklich, dass diese Töne nicht mehr störend wirkten, als die einer Glocke oder eines Tamtam, welche die Accorde einer Symphonie begleiten. — Die Töne des Teponaztli dienten also als eine Art imperfecter Contrabass: die Tonhöhe wechselte mit der Grösse des Instruments, blieb aber der Natur der Sache gemäss in einem und demselben Instrument sich immer gleich, folglich konnte der Teponaztli nicht mit dem Huehuetl, d. h. in verschiedenen Tonlagen, zusammen gestimmt werden. — Die Spitzen der beiden Schlägel wurden mit Wolle oder elastischem Gummi versehen. Der Teponaztli diente als Begleitung zu den historischen Gesängen, wurde auch in den Tempeln bei manchen religiösen Ceremonien und bei fast allen grösseren Bällen und Festen gebraucht.[3]) In Guatemala wurde der Tun vor einer wichtigen kriegerischen Unternehmung mit Blut, welches die Indianer mittelst Dornenstichen von sich selbst zogen, bestrichen; ihre Waffen wurden auf gleiche Weise geheiligt.[4])

---

laufende Einschnitte gemacht wurden. [Woher denn aber zwei verschiedene Töne?]

1) Nebel.

2) Ixtlilxochitl, Histoire des Chichimèques, ch. LXVII.

3) Acosta, lib. VI, cap. XXVII; Oviedo, p. 1, lib. V, c. I; Herrera, dec. I, lib. III, cap. I; u. a. m.

4) Brasseur. — [Nach H. H. Bancroft (vol. I, p. 199) besitzen die Nootka (Columbia Fluss)-Indianer eine Art Pauke aus einem dicken, von unten ausgehöhlten Holzbrett gemacht, auf welchem man mit zwei Schlägeln spielt; — vielleicht eine alte Form des Teponaztli?]

Der Tunkul in Yucatan ist nach Stephens[1] dasselbe Instrument, welches den Eingebornen zur Zeit der spanischen Eroberung bekannt war. Er besteht aus einem hohlen circa drei Fuss langen Holzscheite, über dessen Ende ein Stück Pergament gezogen wird, auf welches der Spieler, die Pauke unterm linken Arm haltend, mit der rechten Hand schlägt. [Brasseur, jedenfalls durch die Aehnlichkeit der Wörter verleitet, meint, dieses Instrument sei dasselbe wie der Tun oder Teponaztli.[2]]

Unter den wilden Indianern findet man eine Unzahl Pauken und Tambourins in den verschiedensten Gestalten; von diesen werden nachstehend nur einige angeführt.

Die Pauke der Irokesen ist nur ungefähr sechs Zoll hoch und fünf breit, wie ein kleines Fass mit fast geraden Seiten, und hat an jedem Ende einen hölzernen Reif; über das obere Ende wird ein Stück Kalbfell gezogen und vom Reif festgehalten. Der Boden ist von Holz, der Schlägel von Eichenholz, ca. $7^{1}/_{2}$ Zoll lang. Die Pauke wird im Weibertanz, im Vogeltanz und den verschiedenen Kriegstänzen gebraucht. Durch ein kleines, unten an der Seite befindliches Loch, welches während des Spielens fest zugestopft bleibt, wird etwas Wasser zum Anfeuchten des Trommelfells hineingegossen. Das vom Verf. untersuchte Exemplar gab den Ton klein *a* an.

Die Pauke der Crees (kris) ist in ihrer Gestalt einem Tambourin sehr ähnlich, hat oft einen Durchmesser von über drei Fuss, ist aber wenig tief; der Ueberzug ist von der Haut des Mussthiers, mit Bildern von Menschen und Thieren kunstlos bemalt. Ein Stock dient als Schlägel. [Franklin, cap. III.]

Die Pueblo-Indianer machen ihre Pauke aus einem ausgehöhlten Baumstamm, ungefähr $2^{1}/_{2}$ Fuss lang und 15 Zoll breit, beide Enden mit einer gegerbten Haut überzogen; sie wird mit zwei Schlägeln gespielt. [H. H. Bancroft, vol. I, p. 552.]

Die Cherokees, Choctaws und Chickasaws brauchten zwei

---

[1] Begebenheiten auf einer Reise in Yucatan, Leipzig, 1853, Cap. VII.
[2] Grammaire de la langue Quiché, Essai, page 9.

Pauken in der Form von irdenen Töpfen, über welche eine dünne, angefeuchtete Rehhaut gespannt wurde; auf diese schlugen die beiden lärmenden Musikanten mit Stöcken, welche bei den religiösen und kriegerischen Festen zugleich mit den Ratteln als Begleitung zu den Gesängen gebraucht wurden. [Adair.]

Das Tambourin der Twanas ist von Holz, viereckig, ein bis zwei Fuss lang und breit, mit einer Tiefe von drei bis fünf Zoll; es ist mit Rehhaut überspannt, deren lederne Zugriemen, sich auf der Unterseite kreuzend, von der linken Hand gehalten werden, während die rechte Hand oben schlägt. Der Ton wechselt der Grösse des Instruments nach zwischen dem einer kleinen Trommel und einer Heerpauke.

Die Assiniboines, Chippewas, Sioux und Montana Indianer haben ähnliche Tambourins, nur rund anstatt viereckig.

Ratteln oder Klappern werden ebenfalls unter allen Indianervölkern in den verschiedensten Formen gefunden.

---

**b. Blasinstrumente.** Das Flageolet [Tafel II, Fig. 1] scheint unter allen Indianernationen einheimisch zu sein. Es wird aus Ceder-, Sumach- oder Holunderholz gefertigt; die beiden letzten werden wegen des leicht zu entfernenden Marks vorgezogen. Man wählt einen Ast oder Stamm der einen Durchmesser von 1 bis $1\frac{1}{4}$ Zoll und eine Länge von 15 bis 20 Zoll hat; er wird der Länge nach halbirt, und jede Hälfte bis $B$ [s. Tafel] und von $B$ bis $A$ ausgehöhlt; die Hälften werden nun zusammengeleimt, und in die obere Hälfte vor und hinter $B$ ein viereckiges Loch [$C$, $D$] durchgeschnitten; vier bis acht Tonlöcher werden hineingebrannt. Eine Holz- oder Metallplatte [$E$] wird über die viereckigen Löcher $C$ und $D$ gelegt, sodass der darin befindliche länglich viereckige Einschnitt genau zu diesen passt; über die Platte wird ein hölzerner Aufsatz [$F$] gebunden; dieser ist unten platt, oben nach Belieben fantastisch geschnitzt; häufig wird vor dem in diesem Aufsatz gemachten Einschnitt ein vibrirender Holz-

oder Metallstreifen gebunden. Der Ton verschiedener Instrumente variirt sehr; für gewöhnlich ist er dem der D-Flöte ähnlich, allein der tiefste Ton (mit allen Tonlöchern geschlossen) ist oft rauh und unangenehm. Das Prinzip der Tonerzeugung ist dasselbe, wie in unserer gewöhnlichen kleinen Pfeife. Die Stimmung ist selten eine reine; in den meisten Fällen die ersten vier bis sechs Stufen der Molltonleiter mit (obgleich nicht in jedem Instrument) deren Octaven. Dieses Flageolet wird stets als Soloinstrument und am häufigsten von jungen Männern gebraucht, die ihren Geliebten ihr zärtliches Gefühl auf diese Weise kundthun wollen.[1] Um die Geliebte aus ihrer Hütte hervorzulocken, spielt der Freier eine ihm eigenthümliche Melodie, welche von keinem andern gespielt wird. Das Flageolet wird oft mit bunten Bändern oder Lederriemen, rohen Malereien u. s. w. geschmückt.

Die Flöte [das Flageolet wird oft irrthümlich Flöte genannt] wird seltener unter den wilden Indianern gefunden. Tafel II, Fig. 2 zeigt eine apache Flöte mit drei Tonlöchern. Die Pueblo-Indianer sollen ihre Tänze und Gesänge mit Flötenmusik begleiten; zuweilen sollen sogar 5 oder 6 Spieler auf Flöten von verschiedenen Grössen zusammenspielen [H. H. Bancroft, vol. I, p. 552, Foot-note]; hierüber fehlt aber jede weitere Bestätigung.

Die Pans-Pfeife (Syrinx) wird unter einigen wilden Indianervölkern in Mexiko und Centralamerika gefunden. [Unter den Peruvianern erreichte dieses Instrument einen hohen Grad der Vervollkommnung. Vergl. Dr. Traill, On a Peruvian Musical Instrument, in Trans. of the R. S. of Edinburgh, vol. XX; auch Garcilasso, wie oben.]

---

[1] Die Irokesen brauchen das Flageolet zu diesem Zweck, obgleich sie keine Liebeslieder haben; — es war auch unter den Peruvianern gebräuchlich; s. Garcilasso de la Vega, Histoire des Incas, Amsterdam, 1637, p. I, lib. II, cap. XXVI. — Ueber das Flageolet der Mexikaner schreibt Nebel: »L'instrument le plus complet, et qui ne laisse presque rien à désirer, c'est leur flageolet. Il compte toute une octave, mais sans les demitons, soit parcequ'on ne les distinguait pas, ou qu'on ne savait pas les rendre. Ils étaient en terre cuite.« [Mit Abbild.]

Unter vielen Indianernationen an der Pacificküste werden Pfeifen von zwei, in Form des Buchstaben V zusammengebundenen Röhren in gleicher Länge gefunden (bisweilen auch mit drei Röhren), die mit dem Mund oder der N a s e geblasen werden. [H. H. Bancroft.]

Ausser diesen Blasinstrumenten giebt es kleine Pfeifen (Kriegspfeife und dergl.), und an der Pacificküste Instrumente von Holz, die einen schnarrenden, ohrzerreissenden Ton von sich geben.

[Die Mexikaner hatten verschiedene von den alten spanischen Schriftstellern oft, jedoch nur flüchtig, erwähnte Blasinstrumente, wie Schalmeyen (Zampoñas), Krummhörner oder Zinken (Cornetas), Hörner (Cuernos), Schneckenmuscheln (Caracoles), Pfeifen (Chiflatos); von den kleinen thönernen Pfeifen werden noch viele gefunden; Nebel meint, sie hätten nur zwei Töne; im Smithsonian Institute befindet sich aber eine, welche die fünf ersten Stufen der Durtonleiter angiebt. Der Ton ist dem der italienischen Ocarina sehr ähnlich, wie auch ihre Gestalt. — Die übrigen Blasinstrumente wurden für Solo- und Zusammenspiel benutzt; diese Musik soll aber nach europäischen Begriffen wenig angenehm gewesen sein. (Torquemada, t. I, lib. II, cap. LXXXVIII.)

c. **Saiteninstrumente.** Diese werden von keinem der alten Schriftsteller (über die Mexikaner) erwähnt, obgleich die Schlag- und Blasinstrumente zuweilen ausführlich beschrieben werden und von diesen letzteren häufig gesprochen wird. Unter den wilden Indianern werden Saiteninstrumente fast gar nicht gefunden; die Apaches haben den H a r p o n[1]), mit einer Saite, und sollen ihre Gesänge damit begleiten. Adair fand ein eigenthümliches Instrument dieser Gattung; die Beschreibung desselben muss mit seinen eigenen Worten gegeben werden. Er nennt es »one of their old sacred musical instruments. It pretty much resembled the Negroe-Banger [banjo] in shape, but far exceeded it in dimensions; for it was about 5 feet long,

---

1) Der spanische Name des Instruments (auf deutsch Harpune), welcher sich auf die eigenthümliche Gestalt bezieht.

63

and a foot wide at the head part of the board, with 8 strings made out of the sinews of a large buffalo. But they were so unskilful in acting the part of the Lyrick, that the Loache, or prophet, who held the instrument between his feet, and along side of his chin, took one end of the bow, whilst a lusty fellow held the other; by sweating labor they scraped out such harsh jarring sounds, as might have been reasonably expected, by a soft ear, to have been sufficient to drive out the devil if he lay any where hid in the house.«

[Die Peruvianer hatten die Tinya, ein fünfsaitiges Instrument; unter den Indianern am Orinocco-Fluss wurden Instrumente mit drei Saiten (»Rabeles«) gesehen.]

# PREFACE

During a stay of some weeks in America in the summer of 1880, the writer was offered the opportunity of visiting the Senecas, an Indian tribe of Iroquois stock living in western New York, and, through this visit, of achieving the real aim of his journey. Here he attended not only the various festivities that are organised annually among the Indians at the time of the harvest festival, but also persuaded one of the most skilled singers to perform for him, after the festival, some fifty or sixty songs, some of which were chosen as being especially characteristic, and were very carefully transcribed (see Notated Examples nos. I to X). In response to an invitation from the director of the Training School for Indian Youth at Carlisle, Pennsylvania, the writer betook himself there, and, through the kind offices of the officials, was enabled to add to his collection a further twenty-two songs from various Indian tribes. These thirty-two songs (nos. I-XXXII of the Notated Examples), discussed in sections 3 to 6, constitute the essential core of this monograph. The remaining paragraphs serve primarily to indicate the meaning this music holds for the Indians, and should in no sense be considered exhaustive. Indian poetry alone would be a valid subject for an extensive work; to describe the innumerable dances and ceremonies of every kind in which music is used would lead us much too far from our subject. The writer has therefore contented himself with drawing attention to the various sources in which, he believes, justification for the general character of certain of his observations may be found.

I avail myself of this opportunity to express my warmest thanks to the following ladies and gentlemen who assisted me by word and deed in the preparation of this monograph: my dear mother Mrs. Elizabeth Hunt, Mrs. H.S. Caswell, Miss H.L. Garratt, Rev. Isaac Baird, Mr. Y. Bonillas, Prof. T.W. Chittenden, Rev. J. Owen Dorsey, Rev. M. Eells, Dr. Wills de Hass, Rev. Horace Edwin Hayden, Maj. J.W. Powell, Capt. R.H. Pratt, Rev. A.L. Riggs, Rev. T.L. Riggs, Rev. John Robinson, Gen. David H. Strother, Rev. Father Eugene Vétromile, Rev. J.P. Williamson.

Leipzig, March 1881                                         THE AUTHOR

# 1 INTRODUCTION

Among both savages and civilized people expressions of feeling acquire through music an intensity that cannot be conveyed by words and gestures alone. But while in the civilized world variety of feelings is normal, the savage experiences comparatively few intellectual and physical impulses; hence his language, together with his music – the language of feeling – remains simple and restricted. It would be difficult to say with certainty how the accompanying songs originated, or how they maintained their present form and particular design. The Indian simplifies (to his own way of thinking) the answer to this question by ascribing a supernatural origin[1] to those songs which are used at particular religious festivals, and he believes the newer songs to be based on these models.

2    Some writers are of the opinion that Indian songs were originally a simple imitation of certain birds; they nevertheless show no intellectual relationship between such trite attempts and the true and higher expression of feeling that every music ought to be, and that the music of the Indians certainly is[2]. A much more obvious and legitimate hypothesis seems to be that these melodies are the result of a long evolution in which, at its simplest, are rooted expressions of joy or grief common to all people (see sections 2 and 6). This hypothesis is strengthened by the fact that according to it music rises directly out of the human heart. It is further supported by the actual situation of the music, which, as voiced by the Indians, is observed at its most basic stage of development. In such cases, however, singing seldom appears to be an independent art, but is almost always accompanied by various dances. In their general features, the

3    performances of the different Indian peoples show striking similarities. Franklin[3] gives us the following description of a dance of the Dog-Rib Indians (British North America): 'and immediately they ranged themselves in a circle, and, keeping their legs widely separated, began to jump simultaneously sideways; their bodies were bent, their hands placed on their hips, and they uttered forcibly the interjection *tsa* at each jump'.

Here the dancers move in a circle, as is customary among all Indian tribes at certain festivals[4]. Along with this occurs a very characteristic feature[5], which, like the group-singing, is to be found in almost all musical performances. This is the monotonous repetition in strongly-marked rhythm of one syllable or of a single word, a feature of the most primitive singing through the whole of North America[6]. This communal singing and dancing is the Indian's highest and almost sole form of aesthetic enjoyment, to which he devotes himself passionately, and which in the south, even at the time of the discovery of America, was

4    intensified to such a degree by ritual drinks that the festivals sometimes ended in a state of general inebriation. At religious festivals in the north, on the other hand, the conduct of performers and audience is exemplary. The Indian's aversion to innovations, and his sturdy persistence in customs sanctified by time, are never more clearly apparent than in everything that concerns his religious music. The words, the tunes, indeed even the smallest gestures are regarded as possessing an inviolable sanctity, and having come from their ancestors must be handed down unaltered to their descendants[7]. In the great magic dance of

the Chippewas, the main idea is repeated over and over: 'Thus our fathers did, isn't that so, brothers? The fathers have taught us that, isn't that so, brothers? We hold fast to the good old customs of the fathers! That is what we want, brothers!'[8]. Though new songs are composed in honour of outstanding warriors, or in remembrance of remarkable events, they rarely show departures from the general characteristics already observed[9]. Therefore while musical development has admittedly been very slow, this is not due to any lack of talent; the Indians, when they come into contact with civilization, often make rapid musical progress[10].

The songs of the Indians are divided into seven different categories, according to the character of the ceremonies for which they are used: (1) cabbalistic songs, performed either in strict seclusion and only by initiates into these mysteries, with dancing and crude instrumental accompaniment (see section 8), or more
5 often used by the witchdoctors (medicine-men) for purposes of healing the sick, banishing evil spirits and similar skills; (2) religious songs; these are the most frequent type, and are sung regularly at particular times of the year[11]; (3) historical songs (see section 2); (4) war-songs; (5) laments; (6) love-songs; (7) songs that are sung at all kinds of social gatherings — these frequently have a half-mystical, half-religious character.

All Indian tribes appear to have songs that correspond in development and variety to the character of the people. The savage, warlike Iroquois[12] possess neither historical songs nor love-songs, although both these types are found among neighbouring tribes. Iroquois women do not participate in singing[13]; on the other hand, among the Mexicans, where civilization, and with it music also, has made the greatest progress, women had equal rights with men in this respect (as in many others). Again with the Iroquois, dance-songs are performed by one or two people (or by a choir) who do not dance; with other tribes (the Mexicans in particular) the dancers sing and the dance-leader has only to mark the beat with his drum-strokes. Further discussion of these and other differences is prevented by lack of material and by inaccuracies in what is available; the points that the performances of the various tribes have in common appear, however, to be more numerous and more important than the differences.

6                     2 POETRY: ORIGIN AND DEVELOPMENT


Simple natural sounds such as 'he ya! he!' (no. XXVIII), or several oft-repeated meaningless words such as 'Kanoñ wi-yo' (no. IV), or seemingly unconnected words like 'Friends — stone — always remain firm — forward!' are intimately related to the more highly developed concepts of Indian poetry, and should be considered, in the light of their simplicity and naturalness, as its origin and primary source[15]. The joyful 'he ya! he!' of the Comanche belongs not only to this tribe but is found also among people who live as far apart from one another as the Iroquois[16], Poncas[17] and Tuanas[18]. The sad 'Oh d-da d-da' (oh! oh!) of the last-named[19] occurs indeed in similar songs of other Indian tribes. The transition from such simple exclamations to individual words, and from these to very short sentences, is a simple one, and especially in terms of musical progress, a self-evident one. The savage can be fully satisfied with such

7 incomplete expressions only as long as his intellectual formation as a whole remains underdeveloped. That such simple songs can continue to exist side by side with other more highly developed songs is not only a proof of perseverance in the Indian's character, but shows moreover that such songs are most intimately connected with his sensibilities. They were not to be rejected as something worn out and obsolete as soon as the new and (in the musical context) more accomplished songs were invented, but still retained their attraction, due especially to their naturalness. Among these monotonous songs there are many that are hallowed not only by use, but also by subject-matter; the name of the All Highest is used only in the many religious songs, although with variations[20]. The songs often have a dramatic element, even in their most primitive form. In the first place, it is especially through the vividness of the mime and through the language of gestures that the real meaning of many short phrases becomes clear. Also it has been discovered in more recent times that there lies in the Indians' language a much deeper meaning than has hitherto been supposed[21]; this is even assumed to be the common property of the most diverse wild Indian tribes, understood by all and used reciprocally[22]. Indians who do not

8 understand a word of one another's language continue for hours with these silent conversations, and can in this way engage in the most detailed communication. Since he has at his disposal such powerful support for, or rather supplement to, his words, it is obvious that the Indian needs far fewer words than does the civilized man in order to express everything that happens within and about him. In those shortest sentences the words give only a fixed point of reference around which he can express his whole art of representation[23] with unrestricted freedom. In those cases where the performing dancer makes use only of the language of gestures (as in song no. III of the Notated Examples, in which the words are sung by two 'conductors' seated in the middle of the circle of dancers) the effect is surprising even to the observer unversed in the language of mime. The young warriors, giving themselves totally to the excitement of the moment, perform the most adventurous leaps; they throw their bodies now to the right, now to the left, now forwards, now backwards, with astonishing vehemence. Grinning at one another with bared teeth and black, fiery, wildly rolling eyes, they turn in a moment with lightning quickness, shouting wildly with joy, while all their movements are accompanied by the liveliest gestures of arms and hands. The words 'Wolf runs' find their fullest interpretation in living images; yet even in the fiercest tumult nobody gets away from the beat, which is strongly marked by the heavy stamping of feet. For an important event such as an impending expedition, when it is good to inspire

9 courage in the less impetuous, the warrior shows off all his strength. With slow creeping steps, as if he wished to attack the enemy the very next moment, he goes, tomahawk in hand, round the circle of assembled warriors singing the war-song (no. IX is that of the Iroquois) with manly resolution. Then, striking the painted totem-pole with the tomahawk, he relates in a high-pitched voice and with vigorous expression his earlier deeds of glory[24], and what he remembers of events of previous expeditions. Fired by his speech and by the applause of the others, the hesitant ones now enter the circle and sing the same song

('I go! I go!') with appropriate gestures, by which they make known their intention to join the war-expedition. The former of these two examples [no. III] shows the relationship of the shorter phrases to external nature; the latter [no. IX] how they can originate in events and deeds. Through frequent repetition of the same words, as is often the case, not only can the melodies be further developed and increased in length, but also the performer is given the opportunity of demonstrating to the onlookers his choice of manifold variations, and through these his own skill; the wilder they are, the truer they are to nature.

The Indian's relationship to nature, his life in and direct contact with her, give his spirit the strongest and most lasting stimulus. Out of this inexhaustible source there flows into him, in ever-changing forms, material for thoughts and sensations which make up a large part of his poetry, and whose main charm lies precisely in this directness of action and feeling. His speeches, as well as his poetic creations, show an abundance of most beautiful images borrowed directly from nature; indeed the main distinction between the ceremonial speech and
10 poetry lies in the fact that the latter is learnt and sung, while the former is improvised and spoken. The natural power of feeling is further enhanced by superstition; it is intended as no mere rhetoric when an Indian chief shouts to the assembled warriors: − 'Happy I feel, that your tomahawks thirst after enemy blood, and that your faithful arrows strain impatiently to take their flight through the air'[25]. He believes that arrows and axes are magical, and that a secret life-force exists in some inanimate objects; as he also believes that animals can understand him quite clearly when he addresses them. The poetry rarely has a regular metrical construction, and is therefore (as far as is yet known) to a large extent rather like sung prose. Some writers go so far as to maintain that the few examples known to us of metrical or rhyming verse are the result of a happy accident rather than the consequence of a deliberate attempt. The research projects at present being undertaken by the Smithsonian Institute will shed more light on this interesting subject in a few years' time; meanwhile this writer is of the decided opinion that just as there is a frequently recurring metrical division[26] in the melodies of the Indians, which is the result of a stirring rhythmic feeling, it is to be expected that the same applies also to the poetry, likewise as a result of that rhythmic feeling. This is not a chance occurrence, but a real attempt, though not a highly-developed one, at creating order[27]. Jingles such as:

        no. XI

              O-la-ko-ta
              Ku-wa-ki-ya | pe!

    or no. XXXI

              A ki le
              Li wañ pe

    or no. XIV

11              Ko la ta ku ya ka pe lo
              O ki ci ze ima tan can ye lo
              E ha ka lesh le hañ wa oñ we lo
              E ye ye ye lo

are as pleasing to the savage ear as are ancient lullabies to small children. Such songs are in themselves not important as evidence; they acquire meaning chiefly in association with others that are more highly developed. The following songs are on a higher level:

1. Serenade (Sioux, no. XII)

Shicé, shicé shanté, mashicä,
Shicéla ká shicé napé, mayúsä;
Shicé wancí, yakéshni,
Shicé shanté, mashicä.
Shicéla ká shicé napé, mayúsä.

(Translation is given in the supplement of Notated Examples)

2. The Earthquake[28]

Tu-wip´ pu-a, tu-wip pu-a
A-vwim̀-pai-ar-ru-wip´ pu-a
Tu-rá-gu-ok, tu-rá-gu-ok
Kai-vwa mu-tú-rai-ka-nok.

(In that country, in that country,
In that bright country
Far from here, far from here
The mountain shook with grief.)

3. The Paradox

Wi-giv´-a ka-rí´-ri
Yú-ga-kai-maí-u-uk
Yú-ga-kai-maí-u-uk
Ma-mum̀-pa-ri-tum-pa.

(The ridge of the mountain
Remains forever there,
Remains forever there,
Yet cliffs continue to fall.)

12 The last two songs, from a people whose ancestors, it seems, were closely related to the Mexicans, have a twofold interest for us; all three show something more than a merely accidental combination of words. Still more important are the historical songs of the 'Waphani' or White River Indians; the translator[29] regards them, in their present form, as 'a mere abridgement of more complete annals which, apparently, have since been lost'. The following section is given here because of its unmistakably metrical nature; it was doubtless composed in this way partly because its regularity provides an aid to memory. This quotation begins with the thirteenth strophe of the third song.

13. Amakolen
Nallahemen
Agunuken
Powasinep
Wapasinep
Akomenep

14. Wihlamok kicholen luchundi
Wematan akomen luchundi.

15. Witéhen wémiluen
Wémaken nihillen.

70

16. Nguttichin Lowaniwi
    Nguttichin Wapaniwi.
    Agamunk topanpek
    Wulliton épannek
17. Wulélémil W'shakuppek
    Wémopannek hakhsinipek
    Kítahikan pokhakhopek
18. Tellenchen kittapaki nillawi
    Wémoltin gutikuni nillawi
    Akomen wapanaki nillawi
    Ponskan-ponskan wémuvi Olini.
19. Lowanapi Wapanapi Shawanapi
    Lanéwapi Tamakwapi Tuméwapi
    Elowapi Powatipi Wilawapi
    Okwisapi Danisapi Allumapi.
20. Wemipayat gunéyunga Shinaking
    Wunkénapi.chanelendam payaking
    Allowélendam kowiyey Tulpaking.

13

14

(Translation:

13.  While our ancestors were still travelling over the water, they saw in the east that the Land of the Serpents was bright and rich.

14.  Chief Beaver Wihlamok[30] and the Great Bird Kicholen both said we must go to Akomen, the Island of Serpents.

15.  You come with us, thus may we exterminate all the Serpent People.

16.  Those from the North and those from the West, all in agreement, went across the water of the frozen sea to take the country.

17.  It was a remarkable sight as they all proceeded over the smooth dark water of the frozen sea at the entrance to the Sea of Serpents, into the great ocean.

18.  There were ten thousand in the darkness, who all left in the dark of one single night, everyone on foot, for the Island of Serpents in the eastern land of Wapanaki.

19.  They were the manly North, the manly East, the manly South; with manly Eagle, manly Beaver, manly Wolf; with manly Hunter, manly Priest, manly Rich One; with manly Wife[31], manly Daughter, manly Hound.

20.  All having arrived there, they remain in the pineland of Shinaking; but those from the west, finding the crossing doubtful, preferred to remain in the old Land of the Tortoises.)

Little is known with certainty about the diffusion of these songs which are of the greatest importance for the history of the Indian. The Spaniards' voyages of discovery showed that the original inhabitants of Haïti, Cuba[32], Yucatan[33], Mexico[34] and a part of Central America[35] possessed such songs. According to Rafinesque[36], the Shawanis, the Illinois and almost every Linapi tribe likewise had such songs, so that one can truly call them national.

# 3 VOCALIZATION AND PERFORMANCE

In this short section only songs nos. I to XXXII will be discussed, from the point of view of their unusual features of vocalisation and performance.

**a. Consonants.** *B, d, f, h, k, l, m, n, p, r* and *t* are pronounced as in German; *c* = tsch; *g* is always hard; *h* is a harsh guttural sound; *j* is as in the French word *je*, and *n̄* as in the French *non̄*; *s* = ss; *sh* = sch; *w* and *y* are almost like *u* and *i* respectively, except that for accurate pronunciation a somewhat stronger contraction of the lips and throat is required than in the case of the former simple vowels; *z* is pronounced as in the French *zèle*.

**b. Vowels.** In the Seneca songs *a* is pronounced as in *Vater*; in those of the Iowas and Kiowas it often has a darker colour, between *a* and the Italian *o*, although in speech this feature is less noticeable. In the remaining songs it is
15 pronounced as by the Senecas. The *a* is the short *ă* of French and English *(patte, pat)*; when combined with *n* it is pronounced like *ain* in *pain*. The *ä* sounds like the German *ä*. *E* is almost always like *é* in French (= *ee* in German *See*), occasionally somewhat broader when sung; it is short only in the case of a quick transition or in staccato passages.

The *i* is always long (= *ie* in German *Kiel*). *O* combined with *n̄* sounds as in the French *non*; *ō* is the broad Italian *o*. Otherwise this vowel has the sound of *oo* as in the German *Boot* except in quick transition and staccato passages, where it resembles the *o* in *soll*. *U* is like *u* in the German *Hut*. The intonation of all vowels is full, somewhat on the broad side, but yet pure and clear; by this means the effectiveness of the songs is considerably enhanced. Most syllables end with a vowel, or with consonants such as *n* and *n̄* which act as a light transition from one pitch-level to the next. This gives the songs a melodious, flowing character, while the strong forward-moving rhythm prevents them from becoming over-sweet. The initial consonants are sometimes pronounced with a clear separation from the accompanying vowels, as in nos. XVI and XVII *(t'o)*, or in no. XXX *(g'li, t'eon̄)*. The syllables are frequently chosen just for their euphony, 'in order to make a good song', said the Seneca A-o-don-we. (Examples of this are the two women's dance-songs nos. IV and V.) Meaningless syllables are sometimes appended, for the sake of their euphony, to those lines in which the meaning of the remaining words is clear, and is therefore not at all changed by this addition[37]. Doubling of the vowel sometimes occurs, in which case it should be exceptionally strongly accented (*ni-i* in song no. III; *a-a* in no. IV).

**c. The Voice Range** of the Indian is, so far as the writer has experienced, not less than that of the white man, that is, of course, when comparing un-
16 trained voices in both cases (this refers only to men). The songs are sung almost without exception in the upper (baritone) register; but most performers had the ability to sing down to low *F* full voice; the writer heard no one who could not reach tenor *f'* with ease. A choir of seventeen young men sang no. IV a whole tone higher than that given in the notated examples below, and they sang the higher notes not at all falsetto but with a full chest voice. The range of the male voice would be, on average, over two octaves, from low *F* to tenor *f'*, or from low *A* to tenor *a'*.

**d. Manner of Performance.** This is highly ingenuous, in accordance with the nature of the poetry and the tunes; the singers appear to feel no need for

72

crescendo and diminuendo, accelerando and ritardando. What the tunes lose through this in sentimental feeling, they gain in natural freshness and the obvious enjoyment which their performance gives to the Indian. There is not much to be said about the quality of the voices; the writer did not find them any more unpleasant than those of (altogether) untrained whites. On the contrary, since among the Indians everybody has a certain amount of practice in singing, and the intervals are sung with certainty and clarity, the impression given by these performances is rather a pleasing one. Some singers who were most skilled in manner and style had really soft, melodious voices. Their certainty of intonation and of rhythmic feeling, together with the complete devotion of everyone involved, form the principal merits of their manner of performance[38].

**e. Performance-Styles and Ornamentation.** As far as the latter is concerned the unchanging short appoggiatura occurs the most frequently. it is always strongly accented. The following example is taken from song no. III:

The *Nachschlag*[a] occurs not infrequently, though not as often as the appoggiatura. This example is taken from the same song:

The only example of a double appoggiatura is likewise to be found in no. III:

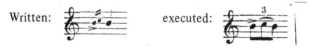

The descending slide (the ascending one does not occur) is found in song no. XIV:

The small notes are not articulated separately and clearly, but quickly at one stroke, rather like an inferior singer in our culture, who, instead of taking an interval cleanly, causes the intervening notes to be heard unclearly, due to his uncertainty. In the case of the Indian songs, however, this feature is deliberate and is consequently performed with more clarity, and in *portamento*; the slide in no. X is executed like a cry of joy. Growling or humming, produced by closing the teeth, has sometimes a remarkable effect, as for example in song no. XIV (scalp-dance), bars 8 and 9, where the sudden g sharp and the slide down to e produced a truly horrifying effect. The slide and the growl are performance-characteristics typical of the savage.

a. In English music of the seventeenth century this term was translated as an *acute* or a *springer* (J.A. Westrup and F.Ll. Harrison, *Collins Music Encyclopedia,* London and Glasgow 1959).

In this section and the following two, only songs nos. I to XXXII will be subjected to a detailed analysis; the remainder will be referred to only for purposes of comparison.

With one exception (no. IX), these thirty-two songs were sung in unison, whether performed by men or by women, or, as in some cases (e.g., nos. XXXI and XXXII), by both together. On the whole, the great majority of Indian songs are alike in character[39]; polyphonic songs are rarely found, and, to judge from the few descriptions of such cases, the harmonic structure of such songs is changed on repetition at the singer's discretion, in such a way that the accompanying voices, while harmonising more or less well, show no strong feeling for harmony. Even the Mexicans were not acquainted with polyphonic singing[40], although their singing is sometimes accompanied by harmonising instruments. Such accompaniment is not found among the wild Indians[41]. An instrument such as the Greek lyre, which even in its least perfect form exercised great influence on the development of harmony by the simultaneous sounding and influence on the development of harmony by the simultaneous sounding and

19    accurate tuning of its strings, was equally unknown to both groups in question. The wild Indian has nevertheless advanced so far in the primitive practice of his art as to be able to recognise aurally the simple tonal relationships within the diatonic scale, and consequently to sing in tune and with assurance most of the intervals in that scale. Hence there arises the question whether there exists in these melodies a strong point of reference, a tonal centre that can be recognised by Indians and civilized people alike, and with respect to which the musician can determine the tonal character of the notes [orig. 'the character of the tonalities'], and name the intervals involved. Song no. IX gives us some information on the Indian's point of view; here the $f$ sung by the choir of warriors appears to be a tonal centre chosen consciously and unanimously[42]. The musician's ear would choose, from the unaccompanied melodic passage, the same note as tonal centre, but would not by any means be satisfied with its monotonous repetition, since this permits no consideration of other latent harmonies (as for instance the dominant seventh chord in bars 2-3 and 11-12). Another example of a consciously selected tonal centre is found in the thanksgiving-song in section 7, no. 3 (orig. p. 46), where the leader sings the melody and the choir always answers with the tonic $f$. Both are Iroquois songs; in the case of this tribe, one may assume with certainty that the singers recognise the existence of a tonal centre in their melodies. This assumption is further supported by even a superficial consideration of songs nos. I to VIII; it can be applied to those other groups represented here by songs, who have in other respects developed as far, or even further.

20    As regards how far harmonic sensitivity may be ascribed to the Indian, it is not possible to state with any certainty which subsidiary notes, apart from the tonic, may enter into his consciousness. However, since: (1) he uses no vocal accompaniment to his songs, except for no. IX; (2) he never has a harmonising instrumental accompaniment to his songs, although, as with the Iroquois, his drum does possess a definite and easily recognisable pitch, and he also has a flageolet at his disposal; (3) in the above-mentioned cases he makes use only of

the tonic, even in places where to the musically trained ear a modulation has occurred; and finally (4) since unison singing without any harmonic vocal or instrumental accompaniment is an essential feature of Indian songs in general and of the appended Notated Examples in particular, every melody in which no passing accidentals appear (i.e., those countermanded by others) is analysed here as though it always remained within the same tonality, therefore without any change of tonal centre. In the writer's opinion, no harmonic accompaniment modulating in the modern fashion could be adapted to suit these melodies; there is thus little scope left for subjective fantasy (or arbitrariness?), and all the more for unprejudiced, objective observation. With this reservation, one may search at will for latent harmonies.

In most cases the tonal centre[44] can be determined without difficulty, especially in those cases where the sixth and seventh degrees of the scale (which often give the tunes a specific colouring) are absent. The following tunes are in this category: nos. I, with tonic $g$; III, with tonic $a$; IV, with tonic $g$; IX, with tonic $f$; XI, with tonic $c$; XX, with tonic $f$; XXIV and XXV, with tonic $c$; XXVI, with tonic $b\,flat$; XXVIII, with tonic $g$; and XXXI, with tonic $d$. These tunes, with the exception of nos. IX and XX, where the third is absent, can be denoted simply as major or minor, since the minor second does not arise, and fourths and fifths are always perfect. In a few simple cases the tonal centre is determined either by the melodic contours or the melodic accent, or by both of these together.

a. The melodic contours are the true determinants in the choice of tonic for the following: no. II, with tonic $a$, in which the succession of notes $e'\,c'\,a\,e'\,c'$ $a\,e^{45}$ remains the determining factor despite the repeated emphasis on $g$, which is related to $e$ as a minor third and to $a$ as a minor seventh, and which always returns to the tonic either directly or through the formulae $g\,b\,e'\,c'\,a$ (bar 10) and $g\,e'\,a\,(e')$ (closing bars); no. VIII, with tonic $c$ where the formulae $e'\,c'$ (bars 1 and 2), $c'\,g$ (bar 4) and $e\,c'\,c'\,e$ (bars 7 and 8) give the whole song the character of a major tonality, which is in no way altered by the formulae $e\,g$ and $g\,e$ (bars 10 and 11), and the repeated emphasis on $e$ at the end; no. XV, with tonic $c'$; in this the pattern $g'\,f'\,d'\,c'$ (bars 3 and 4), like the analogous bars in no. IX (bars 2, 3 and 4), together with $g\,c'$ (bar 11) where the fifth proceeds to the tonic, is decisive in the selection of a tonic; and so furthermore are nos. VII and XII, with tonic $c'$, XIV, with tonic $a$, XVIII, with tonic $g$, XIX, with tonic $e'$, XXI, with tonic $c'$, XXVII, with tonic $d'$, and XXX, with tonic $g$.

b. In the following tunes, the tonic is determined by the melodic accent: nos. XVI and XVII, with tonic $d$, which in both cases makes its presence felt by repeated emphasis at the close. In these two examples the melodic formulae are not sufficient for designating the tonic; that both begin with a second is striking, but in no. XI, where the tonic is undoubtedly $c$, this is also the case (compare no. XXXI, bar 10), and again in no. XXXII, which has a tonic $g$. Here, at the beginning (bars 4, 5 and 6), one might be inclined to choose $c$ as the tonic, as seems indicated by the melodic formulae, but this $c$ does not appear to provide a sufficiently strong point of rest, as does the tonic in other tunes, but is used only in passing.

c. The tonic is determined in the following tunes by the relationship between the accent and the melodic line: no. XIII, with tonic $e$, XXII, with tonic $c'$, XXIII, with tonic $b\,flat$, and XXIX, with tonic $e\,flat$. In this last example the accent falls on *g, e flat* and *b flat* in the most obvious way, whereby the other notes appear as passing notes. Consequently the former have the implications of the main or tonic chord; that this tune ends on the sixth degree of the scale is a remarkable deviation from the practice observed in other tunes.

Once the tonal centre of any tune is determined, one can proceed to an examination of the interval ratios and to naming the tonalities. A glance at the 'Table of Intervals' at the end of this monograph will show that all seven degrees of the diatonic scale are rarely found in any one of these short tunes, that not only the tonic but also the fifth occurs in every tune[46], and that in all cases the latter is sung as a perfect interval. The third degree of the scale occurs in twenty-five tunes, the major third in twenty-one cases and the minor third in four. The fourth occurs in twenty-two tunes, and with one exception is always the perfect fourth. The sixth is found in fifteen tunes, and is always major, while the seventh occurs in eight tunes, in five cases as a minor seventh, in two as major, while in one example both are found.

Some very mistaken ideas about the harmonic nature of Indian songs have become widespread. On the one hand it is maintained that due to their harmonic and rhythmic deviations from the modern note-system it is not possible to transcribe the tunes in our notation; on the other hand it is felt that the modes can be compared to those of the Persians and [Asiatic] Indians, both in number and in interval-ratio. As regards the first opinion, it may be noted that 23 the author was not satisfied merely to sing all of songs nos. I to XXXII, but, having listened to them several times, he sang the same songs through with the Indians. By this procedure it would have been very easy to notice any essential deviation from our system of note-relationships; the writer is convinced of the contrary, namely, that the Indians sing very well in tune, as that word is used by musicians (see also section 6). Against the second opinion the following objections may be raised: (1) the infrequent use of the semitone and the complete avoidance of a smaller interval; together with (2) the extremely sparing use of accidentals; and consequently (3) the clearly diatonic nature of the great majority of tunes. These factors limit, comparatively speaking, the number of modes employed. The modes in question are, moreover, the result of a natural, artless development by these oriental peoples of a precise and hieratic theoretical system. If, in the case of some tune where this or that degree of the scale is missing, one wished, by reason of this incompleteness, to find a motive for naming a new scale or gamut, then the number of modes would be inconveniently increased, since the Indian indeed appears to avoid certain melodic patterns, but nevertheless no particular degree of the diatonic scale. As far as the use of the semitone is concerned, these scales could much more appropriately be compared to those of the Greeks in the time of Aristoxenos (c. 350 B.C.). These modes of the 'Ancients' were as follows[47]:

|     |                |                         |
| --- | -------------- | ----------------------- |
| 1.  | Mixolydian     | = *B c d e f g a b*     |
| 2.  | Lydian         | = *c d e f g a b c'*    |
| 3.  | Phrygian       | = *d e f g a b c' d'*   |
| 4.  | Dorian         | = *e f g a b c' d' e'*  |
| 5.  | Hypolydian     | = *f g a b c' d' e' f'* |
| 6.  | Hypophrygian   | = *g a b c' d' e' f' g'* |
| 7.  | Hypodorian     | = *a b c' d' e' f' g' a'* |
|     | or Locrian     | = *A B c d e f g a*     |

24

76

Since neither the minor second nor the diminished fifth occurs in any of the tunes before us, it can be assumed that the Mixolydian mode is rarely or hardly ever used by the Indians. The Locrian mode has the same interval-distribution as the Hypodorian. With the exception, therefore, of the Mixolydian and Locrian modes, the 'modes of the Ancients' could be reproduced in the following two octaves of the diatonic scale:

$$c \quad d \quad \overbrace{e \quad f} \quad g \quad a \quad \overbrace{b \quad c'} \quad d' \quad \overbrace{e' \quad f'} \quad g' \quad a' \quad \overbrace{b' \quad c''}$$

while each of the six initial notes is taken as a point of departure or tonic of a new tonality or 'octave species', according to the scale; the slurs indicate the semitones.

The Lydian mode is suitably represented with all its intervals in no. VII, since this tune, like the mode, contains the major second, major third, perfect fourth, perfect fifth, major sixth and major seventh[48].

The Phrygian mode has a major second, minor third, perfect fourth, perfect fifth, major sixth and minor seventh. Among the first thirty-two tunes, none is found in which all the degrees of this scale occur. In three examples (nos. II, XIV and XVII), however, the minor third and minor seventh occur; in no. II the only degrees missing are the fourth (which, with one exception, is always perfect) and the sixth (always major), in no. XIV, the second (major, as a rule) and the sixth are not present, while in no. XVII only the sixth is missing. Moreover, nos. XXXVII and XXXVIII are in this mode, so that it seems justified[49] to assume that occurrences of the Phrygian mode are not rare in Indian music, especially since the major sixth and minor seventh are favourite choices of the Indians (see 'Table of Intervals').

The Dorian mode includes the minor second and does not arise in these tunes.

The Hypolydian mode is not found in its complete form; in no. XXIII the augmented fourth occurred once but was superseded immediately afterwards by the perfect fourth. No change of tonal centre is perceived in the momentary use of an accidental such as here, and likewise in no. XIV, where the major seventh occurs once. In the first case it remains *b flat*, in the second *a*. But the mode suffers an essential change through a semitone shift; by the passing use of the augmented fourth, the expression of lamenting in the song is heightened. One should not fail to recognize that the Indians felt and intended the heightened effect achieved by such an alteration.

The Hypophrygian mode with its major second, major third, perfect fourth and fifth, major sixth and minor seventh is found in its complete form in two examples (nos. V and XV); most tunes with a minor third seem to be in either this mode or in the Lydian.

The Hypodorian mode, with its minor sixth, is not to be found; but yet its existence should not be denied, although, as can probably be assumed, the Phrygian (for reasons already given) is the favourite of the modes containing a minor third.

According to the statement of the Greek theoretician[50], the Lydian, Phrygian and Dorian modes were those constructed first by the Greeks; with the exception of the later modes, these oldest modes of the Greeks correspond strikingly with those of the North American Indians.

In the introductory sections it was stated that the music of the Indians is a true and higher expression of feeling ('higher' as opposed to the trivial imitation of nature). In modern music the choice of mode for the melody of a song depends to a substantial degree on the character of the mood to be expressed through the music, as do also the time signature and manner of performance.

The relationship of the harmony of the major and minor triads to feeling has been dealt with in detail and with sensitivity by Moritz Hauptmann[51]. The use of these triads in purely melodic succession, i.e., as broken chords, is of course subject to the same aesthetic principles. Thus apart from the speed at which a tune is sung, and apart from other idiosyncrasies in the singer's performance, one would expect that for a song intended to arouse a happy, playful or courageous mood, a tonality could be chosen in which the major character was predominant; and that, on the other hand, for sad, sombre or tender songs one would use minor. Fundamentally, primitive man has the same feelings as civilized man, although neither as complicated, nor, by virtue of his simple way of life, in such variety. Allowing for this and for the statement made above concerning the fact that Indian music is a true and higher expression of human feelings, one might be justified in concluding that the Indian, in order to give expression to the same feelings as civilized man, must also make the same choice of tonalities, and, consequently, that his melodies must be constructed exclusively in neither the major nor in the minor modes, but should vary according to the content of the songs. In the following observations, the designation 'Lydian' or 'Hypophrygian' will be replaced by the simpler term 'major' and 'Phrygian' by 'minor', whereby the character of the mode will be indicated with sufficient clarity; for the purpose of better understanding, tempo and manner of performance are also given:

| | |
|---|---|
| I. | Andante; mood mild, religious but serene — *major* |
| II. | Allegretto; thanksgiving-song, with reverence — *minor* |
| III. | Quick, wild, breathless; wolf-dance — *minor* |
| IV & V. | Fast; cheerful dances — *major* |
| VI. | Andante con moto; playful, cheerful — *major* |
| VII & VIII. | Allegretto risoluto; courageous war-songs — *major* |
| IX. | Andante con moto; song of the resolute warrior |
| X. | Andante con moto, mezza voce; deep reverence |
| XI. | Allegro; happy love-dance of several Indian tribes — *major* |
| XII. | Andante con moto; night-song or serenade — *major* |
| XIII. | Very quick; sure of victory, yet friendly — *major* |
| XIV. | Quick; with half-closed mouth, cruelly — *minor* |
| XV. | Fairly fast; a storm-song, beginning happily but with minor ending (minor seventh) — *major* |
| XVI. | Fairly fast; melancholy song of victory, like the next, |
| XVII. | Fairly fast; a kind of prayer for God's protection in battle — *minor* |
| XVIII. | Allegretto; cheerful love-song — *major* |
| XIX & XX. | Allegretto; thanksgiving-dances, happy |
| XXI. | Quick; rejoicing song of victory — *major* |
| XXII. | Fairly quick; women's thanksgiving-song, happy — *major* |
| XXIII. | Not fast; song of a mother to her absent son (augmented fourth), plaintive — *major*[52] |
| XXIV. | Not fast; melancholy love-song, plaintive — *major*[52] |

| XXV & XXVI. | Quick; fiery war-songs — *major* |
| XXVII. | Andante con moto; war-song lamenting the loss of a chieftain — *major* |
| XXVIII & XXIX. | Allegro; happy dance-songs — *major* |
| XXX. | Allegretto; love-song — *major* |
| XXXI. | Allegro; war-song — *major* |
| XXXII. | Lively; gay dance-song — *major* |

It is indeed hardly to be expected that these songs, removed as they are from their naural, savage surroundings, should have the same effect here. Similarly, how different is that precious Alpine flower, the edelweiss, when in its free wind-swept native place, from its situation down in the valley among the multi-coloured garden plants, where it can barely maintain its pitiful existence! Naturally, it is treasured there by no one more than by the one who has picked it himself!

## 5 MELODIC PATTERNS

Every melody has a dual mode of movement: the rhythmic and the inter-
29 vallic[55]. Rhythmic movement will be discussed at length in section 6; the present section, therefore, deals only with the intervallic mode. This again has a dual mode of movement: firstly, stepwise movement, and secondly, leaping movement; both of these, interacting and alternating (separate and independent only in the rarest cases), form the melodic patterns. Now if these last were just a chance occurrence without any appearance of a fixed point of rest or of control in the succession of notes, then it would be merely an unplanned and formless meandering of sounds. However, as has been demonstrated in the foregoing paragraphs, each of these tunes has a firm basis, a tonic, and the fifth is associated with this in each example. The more decided the contrast appears to be between tonic and fifth, the more clearly the character of the tonality emerges, whether through the direct succession of these two degrees or their simple linking by means of the third. In some tunes (nos. I, XIV and XXVIII) only the tonic, third and fifth, i.e., the notes of the tonic triad, are found. In no. II there appears a higher degree of melodic development; here the tune begins on the fifth, *e*, moves through the minor third *c'* to the tonic *a*, and after a repetition of this pattern, falls to the fifth *e*. Still using this as a basis, the tune moves from the tonic chord to the dominant chord *e g (a) b*, then back to *g* and again to the tonic *a* (the minor seventh is used here in both descending and ascending patterns). Then follow the fifth *e*, tonic *a*, minor seventh *g* (= third of the dominant chord), tonic *a* and once again the minor seventh, all strongly accented, the last repeated. From this *g* the tune proceeds through the second *b* up to the fifth *e'*; the dominant chord again appears in this succession of notes. The pattern just described is now repeated and the tune ends on the fifth, following the sounding of the tonic. From this brief summary it follows that not only
30 can the tonic and fifth be introduced at particularly prominent points, but also that the triads based on these two degrees (in the form of the broken chords

*a c e'* and *e g b* respectively) are used only in leaping motion; while it is solely through stepwise motion that a relationship between the two chords, or a transition from one to the other, may be achieved. The following examples of melodic succession, of the progress of the tune from one degree to the next, are taken from the remaining tunes and will clarify the relationship between tonic and fifth. The Roman numeral indicates the number of the tune in question, the letters its tonic, while the Arabic number refers to the bar in which the example in question may be found.

The second, by which is meant the major second in all cases, proceeds: (1) to the tonic, either directly (XI *c* 3) or through the third[56] (IV *g*) or the fifth (XII *c* 10), or the seventh, descending (II *a* 5) or the fourth, back to the second and then directly to the tonic (VI *g* 7); (2) to the third through the fourth (XI *c* 11) or the fifth (XII *c* 21), (3) to the fifth directly (II *a* 10) or through the fourth (XIII *d* 10) or third (XXVI *b flat* 4).

[See notations in the original text, pp. 30-31]

31     In these examples, where the principal features in the treatment of the second degree of the scale are summarised, it can most appropriately be regarded, from its placing in the different melodic lines, as the fifth note from the dominant, i.e., as part of the dominant or dominant seventh chord.

The fourth proceeds: (1) to the tonic, directly (IV *g* ascending, XIII *d* descending) or through the second (III *a* 11) or through the third (III *a* ending) or through the fifth (V *e* 18); (2) to the third, directly (VIII *c* 7) or through the fifth (III *a* 1); (3) to the fifth, directly (V *e* 14) or through the third (III *a* 6).

[See notations in the original text, p. 31]

An immediate following of fourth by sixth or vice versa is not found in any of the tunes discussed, and likewise, rarely is there an indirect relationship between these two degrees (in the sense that they might be regarded as parts of

32 one and the same chord; see XVIII *g* 19). Therefore the subdominant triad (as a broken chord) hardly ever arises; instead, the fourth appears as the root of this chord in cases where it proceeds directly to the tonic, rather as an imperfect, hasty transition from the dominant seventh chord to the tonic chord — the more so when, as in most cases, it is immediately preceded by either the fifth (XIII *d* 13) or the second (XI *c* 36).

The sixth proceeds: (1) to the tonic, directly (VII *c* 10) or through the second (XXX *g* 4 from the end — the only example); (2) to the fifth, directly (V *e* 2) or through the second, ascending (XII *c* 6 from the end — the only example); (3) to the third, directly (XXII *c* 3 — the only example), or through the fifth (VIII *c* 9).

[See notations in the original text, p. 32]

As has been stated above, the relationship of the sixth to the fourth (therefore a third in a possible subdominant chord) is of little importance in these tunes. In several cases, one could indeed interpret a fourth as a subdominant and thus theoretically attribute a subdominant harmony to the tune. However, the facts that this triad does not once occur as a broken chord, and that the fourth and sixth never once appear as directly related degrees, make very problematic the assumption that the Indian really has any concept of the subdominant harmony and that he to some extent adjusts his tune-formations according to it. All the more important is the placing of the sixth as a transi-

tional note between tonic and fifth (ascending) in a succession such as second, tonic, sixth and fifth (or the last three only). In these successions the sixth, as the second degree above the dominant, has the same relationship to the fifth as
33 the second has to the tonic in similar passages (fifth, fourth, second, tonic descending).
[See notations in the original text, p. 33]

Through the frequent use of the sixth as the third below the tonic[57], many melodies achieve a soft, minor quality. This occurs particularly when the third above the tonic is associated with this combination:
[See notations in the original text, p. 33]

The examples already cited have shown so clearly the dependence of the sixth on the tonic and the fifth that it scarcely seems valid to regard it here as the root of a chord recognised by the Indian. Rather, the tonic may be seen as a gravitational point upon which the third and sixth equally depend, as third above and third below respectively.

The seventh degree proceeds: (1) to the tonic, directly (II *a* 4, 5, V *e* 6), or
34 through the fifth (II *a* ending, XVI *a* 9); (2) to the fifth, directly (VII *c* 15, XIV *a* 12), or through the second (II *a* 9):
[See notations in the original text, p. 34]
In one example, it bears no clear relationship to the other notes of the dominant chord; elsewhere its situation as third of the dominant chord is unmistakable.

From this investigation it is evident that the chief function of the second degree is as the fifth of the dominant chord. The fourth appears in most cases as the dominant seventh, and the seventh as third of the dominant chord; these three intervals are employed essentially as parts of the dominant or dominant seventh chord from the fifth, the root of this chord. The third, a component of the tonic chord, depends on the tonic. The fifth sometimes appears as a dominant, as the root of a chord, and sometimes is dependent on the tonic as the fifth of the tonic chord. The situation of this interval in melodic successions is consequently such that it manifests its essential function either in the tonic, as the basis of a broken chord, or in the fifth, as has already been demonstrated in no. II. Whether these two chords are inherent in the mind of the Indian cannot be decided with certainty from the material at hand; but it is clear that the tonic and fifth are real pivots for his tunes. The ambivalent position of the sixth, sometimes drawn to the tonic, sometimes to the fifth, and never being an unambiguous component of the subdominant chord, strengthens this assumption. The few irregularities in melodic line do not furnish sufficient evidence to the contrary. The most striking evidence for the predominant position
35 of the tonic and fifth is provided by the endings of the tunes. Out of thirty-two tunes, sixteen end on the tonic and eleven on the fifth, while one each end on the third and sixth; three are incomplete.[58]


# 6 RHYTHM


The simplest rhythmical form arises out of a succession of pulses, pitches or other audible sounds which follow one another in equal strength and at equal intervals of time. Supposing that such consistently equal periods are marked and articulated by a steady pulse, then only the down-beat needs to have a definite rhythmic character. For if the hand were raised to introduce further beats of rhythmic significance, then this raising of the hand would appear as an upbeat (arsis) and the downbeat as thesis; thereby the single time-impulse is transformed into a double one. Consequently, this first rhythmic impulse, the simple ordering in time, stands between unordered time and the beat. By the concept 'beat' is meant the regular recurrence of a main accent, and this presupposes the existence of a secondary accent. The simplest beat-form, therefore, consists of a primary and a secondary accent, and is consequently binary, while the first rhythmic impulse is unitary.

36    Songs nos. I to XXXII are accompanied by just such monotonous beats, where the performers take account only of the regular succession of down-beats[59]. The beats are marked either with rattles or sticks, on drums or with the foot (in some cases, e.g. nos. IV and V, with the first three together). This method of keeping time is widespread[60] among the Indians, and seems, as far as the experience of the writer goes, to have become almost second nature to the singers, so that they often found themselves unable to sing their songs without such an accompaniment. The chief aim of this noisy, monotonous, rhythmic beat appears to be to keep steady time while crowds are dancing; hence also the large number of time-keeping instruments (see section 9) and their general use. The voices of even the most experienced singers do not possess sufficient power to penetrate the monotonous stamping of the dancers at such great dance-festivals where only a few are singing. This accompaniment is likewise indispensable at festivals where the dancers themselves sing. So far, it has been a question only of marking the rhythm; but of what kind is the relationship between this and the vocal or melodic accent? We have, as it happens, an illustration of this relationship in the dance of the Dog-Rib Indians, mentioned in section 1, which is from the lowest level of the artistic development of the Indian. If one wishes to look for an origin of rhythmic evolution, it is hardly necessary to begin further back in the artistic history of the Indian; this crude dance has an unmistakably primeval character. In the first place, rhythm, everywhere a main factor in Indian social dances, appears here to be the sole object of the whole performance, while the text and melody (?) of the song are com-
37 pletely subordinate. Secondly, the rhythm is not metrical but homorhythmic; and thirdly, no time-keeping instrument is employed. But since the manner and method of marking the rhythm have the same homorhythmic character in those songs before us which are, melodically speaking, relatively highly developed, then the progress in the development of metrical forms from homorhythm is clearly to be sought for in their tune[61]. Thus the song appears initially as though closely tied to the homorhythmic beat, and would seem to be the next step in the rhythmic evolution, whereby the melody acquires somewhat greater freedom of rhythmic movement, in which the sung notes, instead of occurring always with the same accent and at the same time as the beats, could also occur near or between them, or even have 'individual' accents of their own. Song no. X[62], a primeval religious song, illustrates this stage of development.
[See notation in the original text, p. 37]

This song was sung by men only, who trotted around two wooden benches set up in the middle of the dance-hall. The main ('individual') accent is indicated by xx; for every step of their ungraceful, disorderly movement, a rather weak accent is shouted out (just as in the Dog-Rib dance). No. IV offers an example of an extreme case of irregularity in melodic accentuation.

[See notation in the original text, p. 38]

38    Further examples of the most primitive songs may be found in no. XXXIX. Here there is no purely temporary, equally-balanced shifting of accent, as often occurs in melodies that are otherwise in a regular beat; irregularity is more often the rule. The concept of 'metre' is not applicable to this wild and turbulent type of melody; it strives, as it were, to wrest itself free from the burdensome monotony of the rhythmic accompaniment by unusual leaps and violent anticipations and retardations of the accents, but it is nevertheless carried along by the irresistible rhythmic torrent[63].

The balance between rhythm and melody is restored chiefly through the development of metrical form. This may occur in two ways. In the first, the chief melodic accent may coincide with each beat, while the melody, instead of 39 keeping to the simple rhythmic movement of the beats, can maintain duple, triple or quadruple movement, and can therefore (when either a quarter-note or a dotted quarter-note beat is set up) be in 2/8, 3/8 or 4/16 metre. In the second, the chief melodic accent may coincide with every second, third or fourth beat instead of with every beat, whence arise 2/4, 3/4 or 4/4 metre. By these means we have obtained six metrical types of rhythmic movement, examples of all of which may be found among the notated tunes (no. IX is in fact incomplete; the segment given here may be written equally in 3/4 or in 2/8 metre). By deciding on the time-signature according to which a tune should be notated, the listener tries to free himself, as far as is possible, from the feeling of monotony generated by the homorhythmic succession of beats, and to focus his attention as best he can on the melodic accent. However, with this endeavour he soon becomes aware that in many instances the inner conflict between rhythm and melody is not fully resolved, and that rhythmic irregularities frequently recur, as in songs nos. I and II. In order to make their rhythmic peculiarities more comprehensible, there follows here a short description of the Iroquois harvest-festival dance.

The 'dance-house' is a wooden building some fifty feet long and thirty feet wide; it contains one large room, the 'dance-hall', around whose walls two rows of seats are arranged for the onlookers. In the middle of the hall stand two rather long, low wooden benches; the dancers occupy the remaining space. The leading singer, who functions simultaneously as the leader of the whole performance, sits astride one of the wooden benches; opposite him, on the same bench, sits a second singer at such a distance that the large rattles do not knock against each other (each singer holds one rattle in his hand in order to indicate the beat). Those young warriors who take pleasure in dancing move with slow steps in a circle around both singers. The leader now begins to strike with his 40 rattle, which he holds with two hands, on the wooden bench, and is accompanied with the greatest precision by the other singer. At the beginning the strokes come slowly and weakly, but increase progressively in speed and vehemence until the correct tempo is reached. (This is repeated for almost every song at

83

the harvest-festival, as though the singers wanted to collect their thoughts and recall the songs to memory.) Then the leader calls out to the warriors: 'Do you wish to begin?'. They answer, as one man, with a loud cry of assent, and the song begins, at first accompanied by single beats, but soon by double beats, which are performed with such speed that each seems almost to be a single beat. On the repetition of the melody the single beats are employed again, but in such a way that the two persons alternate in striking the wooden bench, while for every second beat the rattle is shaken downwards only, more or less as the conductor of a choir waves his baton when conducting a piece in 2/4 time.

(The single stroke is indicated by X, the double stroke by X and the shaking of the rattle when no stroke occurs is shown by o).
[See notations in the original text, pp. 40, 41]

41     The movement of the dancers' feet corresponds exactly to the character of the strokes; this is true also of their proportions, since only the rhythm, and
42 not the metre, is indicated. At the beginning of each song the dancers lightly balance from one foot to the other for as long as the single beats fall. As soon as the double beats commence, the dancers also begin to perform in double beats, heavily stamping one foot after the other in a controlled fury. The noise is increased by little bells tied round the knee, and it rises to an indescribable din when the dance tempo reaches prestissimo. In no. I a sharp tendency towards a 2/4 beat is observable, though this is not subsequently realised. In no. II the same time-pattern is developed with almost total regularity: one need only re-write the two-beat *b* at the first repetition of the words 'Son gua' as a length-ened quarter-note (X) to make the tune appear completely metrical. The writing of *b* as a half-note is nonetheless more correct, since the time-length of this note corresponds exactly with the time required for two beats. Similar instances may be found in nos. V and XI.

    Returning to the aforementioned time-signatures (2/8, 3/8, 4/16, 2/4, 3/4 and 4/4), the next point to be raised is that out of thirty-two tunes only five are in compound time as opposed to twenty-four in simple time (nos. I, IV and X are not regarded as having any metrical form). Only two of the latter are in 4/4 time, while twenty-two are in 2/8 or 2/4. Of the fifteen tunes in 2/4 metre. thirteen are accompanied by dances in which it is necessary to alternate the feet. Since most songs, especially those of the less developed Indian tribes, are accompanied by dancing, it is by no means unlikely that the 2/4 metre had its origin in this very alternation of the feet, and that it and the 2/8 metre were the original metrical forms[64].

43     In the case of the metrical forms already mentioned, in several tunes a group of bars forms a unit. No. VI is divided into three equal segments or rhythmic sections, each section containing four bars; in no. VII each segment contains four bars and is sharply distinguished from the others; no. IX contains five three-bar sections; no. XVII has nine such sections; no. XXVII contains four sections, no. XXVIII six and no. XXXI eight two-bar sections, while no. XXX has four four-bar sections.

    In the fifteenth song the melodic ictus coincides each time with the word-accent; this is not the case in the other Dakota songs or in the ancient religious songs (such as nos. I, II, III, IV, V, X, XIX, XX, XXXII). Examples such as no X, and especially no. IV, show that the accent can be pulled about in every fashion. The relationship of the word-accent to that of the melody and rhythm, and the origins of the various ways of shifting the accent could be the subject of a very interesting chapter. However, such an analysis can be undertaken with real success only if the researcher has an extensive knowledge of Indian languages, or else an excellent interpreter. The writer has neither of these at his disposal.

44 In the councils of the Iroquois, when these have an official character, every sentence is begun with a rough throat-sound, followed by its upper octave, shouted out with the greatest vehemence. Until the beginning of the next sentence the speech continues on this octave-note and the major second above it, thus:

[See notation in the original text, p. 44]

The word-accent seems always to be on the second, the 'high note'. In the songs, the melodic accent always occurs on a beat or a footstep and, in some of the older songs (such as nos. III and IV), seemingly without regard for the prosodic accent. At all events there is initially more emphasis laid on the rhythmic aspect of the tunes (as an accompaniment to the dances) than on the exact observance of syllable-duration or on the prosodic accent.


## 7 RECITATIVE


The question whether the music of the Indians first had a rhythmically measured form or the unmeasured pattern of recitative is of decided interest. If by 'recitative' we understand those primeval, half-unconscious attempts such as shouting for joy, pitiful laments expressing grief or bodily anguish, or the imitation of birds and of other natural sounds, then recitative could be regarded, without much hesitation, as the older form of music. But if the practice of an art which is still in a rather crude state is in question, then recitative may be regarded in a totally different light. Westphal[65] chooses the former interpretation without further deliberation when he writes: 'The rhythmic and symmetrical in art is older and more natural than the unrhythmic and asymmetrical'. He re-

45 lies on the assertion that a desire for abstract ordering and symmetry is inherent in the human mind. The assumption seems similarly valid in the abstract: recitative springs, as a pure outpouring of the heart, from an inborn musical impulse, and does not need to assume an organised rhythmic form in order to be recognised as art. Westphal says (his section 10): '[Organised] Rhythm is something that is by no means essential to rhythm in the sense of its inner essence, by virtue of which it is the movement-element in the arts of the muses'. As concerns the nature of this element when performed by one person alone, it [i.e., recitative] exists in intimate relationship with, and at the stage of development immediately following the 'attempts' discussed above, and may consequently be regarded as the older form (in contrast with the rhythmic) in musical evolution.

Concerning the relevance of this question to the music of the Indians, the

following observations may be made:

1. The aim of by far the greatest part of the songs of the wild Indians in general (but especially among those less highly developed) is cooperation, and this always appears as something ordered or rhythmic. The Senecas, for example, who have never reached the point of composing love-songs, have produced hardly any songs which were not intended for group singing; even funeral dirges are sung by several women together. All their songs, without exception, have a measured form. The religious dance-songs are those said by the Senecas themselves to be the oldest.

2. An unbroken, step-by-step succession of these rhythmic songs can be produced which ranges from the crudest beginnings to the almost perfect metrical song (see sections 2 and 6).

3. Due to its irregular form, which is left to the discretion of the singer, recitative can be sung only by a solo singer. However, in the simpler examples of those songs which are performed by one person, the melody does have rhythmic movement (see nos. XXXV, XXXIX, XLII, XLIII, also 'Webino' songs 46 figs. 1 and 2 in section 8). On the subject of the cabbalistic songs of the Dakota medicine-men, Professor T.W. Chittenden (Appleton, Wisconsin) has written to the author that they are accompanied by a rattle or a drum (therefore rhythmically). Catlin (p. 370) says that the Dakota uses a soft drum-accompaniment for those songs which he sings to himself when alone in his hut. In a thanksgiving-dance of the Senecas the leader first sang some notes which were of rhythmic significance for him, although they had hardly any connection with the rhythm of the dance; he was answered by the choir on $f'$ (the tonic of his melody):

[See notation in the original text, p. 46]

and so on with little variation.

4. Those same writers who lay emphasis on the rhythmic character of Indian songs say nothing of recitative, but rather, in cases where this song-form might be expected, show those songs to be explicitly rhythmic, e.g., when a warrior sings to the others of his heroic deeds (Loskiel, p. 134). Powers (chap. 2, also pp. 235-7) expressly states that the improvisations of the California Indians are strongly rhythmic.

Improvisations in which this manner of performance (recitative) may occur have a flow of words and a clarity of expression quite incompatible with the idea of a primitive song. This may be observed in death-songs (see Domenech, p. 162) in love-songs (ibid., p. 148), and in improvised songs concerning good 47 or bad news or other themes (see Bancroft, vol. 1, p. 738; also Eels, p. 250).

The available material is insufficient to provide a conclusive answer to this question. However, the facts listed above show that Westphal's conclusion regarding the songs of the Indians is correct, although the reason he offers may be disputed. What does appear to the present writer to be 'in no way necessary' is to deal with this question as an abstract one, and to relegate it *a priori* to the shadowy regions of inborn or 'immanent' ideas, especially when a specific and more easily comprehensible purpose seems to be a valid motive for organised rhythmic movement. Daily life offers us numerous examples of the necessity for organised cooperation. Two people walking together through the town must keep in step so that they do not bump against one another. Every drill-sergeant knows that a feeling for rhythm is by no means inborn in many of his recruits; on the contrary, they learn organised marching only after repeated attempts and some very unpleasant experiences. But how does it come about that among the Indians everybody has a strong feeling for rhythm? First of all, because they have both watched and joined in these dances from earliest childhood; and secondly, because the aspirations of the leader of the round dances to become the most skilful and most graceful leading dancer are continuously reinforced and strengthened by his own personal ambition, and by the example of the most distinguished counsellors and warriors among these savage tribes. The monotony of the simplest rhythmic figure which Professor Westphal finds so unbearable indicates to the savage the necessary points of rest in his performances, as has already been demonstrated. Organised rhythmic movement provides the natural and necessary condition which ensures that these performances can take place in an acceptable manner. That rhythm (even 'of the most elementary kind') appears agreeable to the human spirit, and necessary to the dances of the savages, 48 is certainly no reason for the assertion that it is 'immanent in the human being'. Professor Westphal is of the decided opinion that 'we might without fear put forward the proposition that the origins of poetry (the lyrical category) as outlined here (in section 13) were equally the origins of music'. Thus he assumes that music began at the time when the metrical form of lyrical poetry was perfected! He calls this form 'rhythmic' without seeming to consider that rhythm supplies material for the metrical forms, and can very easily exist without them.

## 8  WRITTEN SYMBOLS

It is unlikely that the symbols given at the end of this monograph bear any direct relationship to the pitches of the melodies. Schoolcraft[66], from whose extensive work these examples have been taken, does not in fact exclude this possibility; he considers, however, that they are not of phonetic but of mnemonic significance in relation to the words of the songs — therefore that the symbols are intended to recall to memory the subjects of the songs. It need not be assumed that, since it has not occurred to these Indians to reproduce in writing simple consonants and vowels, they were not able to invent a system of notation which would preserve the subtly fluctuating pitches of the tunes. The singers attempt rather to reinforce their memories in such a way that they will not lose their presence of mind in the middle of the noisiest dance, but may sing right through their songs without any mechanical aid, and often even in a pre-determined order. A-ō-doñ-wĕ affirmed that he always sings the eighty-nine harvest-festival songs in the same order without having to reflect for a long time. 49 Rev. Eugène Vetromile[67], who devoted special attention to the writing of the Micmacs and related tribes, explicitly states that these Indians could express every thought, even with the most diverse modifications, through the medium of their hieroglyphs. Nevertheless, they had no system of notation, nor any sign that had a relationship to pitch[68]. Rafinesque[69], translator of the painted documents called 'Wallam-Olum', which were found among the Wapahani or White River Indians, is of the opinion that their purpose was to preserve by mnemonic methods the words of these historical songs. He further states: 'The whole thing is purely a catalogue of those of their chiefs who performed outstanding feats, a phenomenon which does not, however, exist in similar documents of the Mexicans' (? )

The six symbols depicted here are the first of thirty which were drawn on a board made of birch-bark; such a board is usually called a 'music board', because songs are sung from it. These symbols are used in certain orgies of a widely dispersed Indian society called 'Webino'[70]; they were arranged on this 'board' in four horizontal lines; the user began at the bottom right-hand corner and read from right to left.

Fig. 1 is the introductory song, and illustrates an Indian hut prepared for the nocturnal dance, decorated with seven crosses which represent seven corpses, and crowned with a magic bone and feathers. One imagines that the hut could move and creep around. He in whose hut the other members of the society have assembled sings alone:

50

| | |
|---|---|
| We bi no | (Webino) |
| Pi mo de | (it creeps) |
| Ni wi gi wam | (my hut) (D.C.) |

Hai ō he
Nhu i we
Nhu i we
He! he! hu! hu! hu!
(My hut creeps around by the power of the Webino)

Fig. 2.  An Indian holds a serpent in his hand. This was caught under the soil by magic power, and is displayed as a triumph of dexterity.

A nō
Muk kum mig
In doan
Di nōn
Nō muk
Kum mig
Hai ō he  etc.
(Under the soil I captured you)

The stroke between figs. 2 and 3 indicates a pause; from this point onwards everyone sings together and the dance begins, accompanied by the usual instruments — drum and rattles.

Fig. 3.  A seated Indian, crowned with feathers, holds a drumstick in his outstretched hand.

Gai e nīn (Gai-e = also)
Ni we bi no
Hai! e! i!  (D.C.) (cabbalistic)
(I also am a Webino)

Fig. 4.  A spirit dancing on part of the arc of heaven; the horns would signify either a spirit or a Webino overcome by the power of a spirit.

We bi no
Nō ni mi ō (D.C.)
Hai! e! i!  etc. (cabbalistic)
(I call the Webinos to dance)

51    Fig. 5. A magic bone decorated with feathers; a symbol of the strength it possesses to move through the air as though winged.

> Ki jig
> I mi
> In gi
> Ne osh
> Shi an
> Hai! e! i!  etc. (cabbalistic)

(Through the sky! through the sky I soar!)

Fig. 6. A large serpent, 'gitchy kinebik', which, as in this case, is always depicted with horns; it is the symbol of life.

> Mon i do
> Wi ōn
> E ko
> We bi no
> Nuk ke yōn
> Hi! e!  etc.

(I am a Webino spirit; this is my work)

## 9 INSTRUMENTS

**a. Percussion instruments.** These, in their various forms, have the widest distribution, and are not wholly lacking in any Indian tribe. However, only in Mexico, Central America and the Hispanic islands did they have a definite pitch which harmonised with the human voice or other instruments. The most highly developed instrument of this kind was the HUEHUETL (huehuitl, vevetl,[72] tlapanhuehuetl[73]), a type of drum used in Mexico and Central America. The
52 huehuetl consisted of a cylindrical, hollowed-out wooden block that was carved and painted on the outside, was three to four feet tall and as thick as a man, and stood upright on a tripod. The upper end was covered with leather or parchment that could be made more or less tense, and accordingly produced a higher or lower pitch. It was struck with the fingers, and this required great skill. This instrument was frequently played with the teponaztli and, if we may believe the early Spanish historians, in complete harmonic accord with that instrument (see paragraph on the teponaztli below). Torquemada states that the difference in pitch of the huehuetl from the edge to the centre of the drumhead is a fifth (*hace su diapente*, lit. 'makes its fifth'), that the instrument was played in such a way as to exploit its variety of timbre and pitch *(por sus puntos, y tonos)*, and that the pitches were sometimes higher, sometimes lower, in tune with the songs[b]. According to this account the drum accompaniment was apparently a harmonising bass.

The word TEPONAZTLI (teponaztle, tepunaztli), according to Brasseur[74],

---

b. For full text and English translation of this passage see Frank Harrison, *Time, Place and Music* (Amsterdam 1973), pp. 33, 44.

is derived from the word *teponovoz* in the Quiché language. This is the same instrument as the TUN, and is still used today by the natives in Mexico and Central America[75]. It was always made of hard wood, often very beautifully carved. In its simplest version, it retained the form of a two- to five-foot[76] length of tree-trunk[77], while in its more artistic version it was worked into an almost square shape. It was hollowed out from below, in such a way, however, that the two ends still retained a thickness of three to four inches, while at the centre three incisions were made, two along the length of the block and the third between them, so that the three together formed the character ⊒⊏ Each of the tongues produced in this manner was a few millimetres thick[c]. When struck with drumsticks, two different pitches were produced which, in different instruments, were a third, fourth, fifth, sixth or octave apart[79]. The sound of the teponaztli was very loud and often euphonious[80]; it could sometimes be heard at a distance of several miles. In the music for the dance-drama 'Rabinal-Achi' the tun definitely seems not to harmonise with the two trumpets. However, in the preface to his *Grammaire* Brasseur expressly states that these sounds were not any more disturbing than that of a bell or a tamtam which accompany the chords of a symphony. The sounds of the teponaztli served therefore as a kind of imperfect double-bass[d]. The pitch varied with the size of the instrument, though in the nature of things it always stayed the same in any one instrument; consequently the teponaztli could not be tuned to conform to the huehuetl, i.e., to its different pitch-levels. The tips of the two drumsticks were furnished with wool or elastic. The teponaztli was used as an accompanying instrument in the performance of historical songs, and was also employed in the temples for some religious ceremonies, and at almost all the greater dances and festivals[81]. In Guatemala, before an important war-making expedition, the tun was smeared with blood that the Indians drew from themselves by means of thorns. Their weapons were consecrated in the same way[82].

The TUNKUL in Yucatan, according to Stephens[83], is the same instrument as that known among the natives at the time of the Spanish conquest. It consists of a hollow wooden log about three feet in length over which a piece of parchment is drawn on which the player beats with his right hand, while he holds the drum under his left arm. (Brasseur, apparently misled by the similarity of the words, is of the opinion that this instrument is the same as the *tun* or teponaztli.)

An immense number of DRUMS and TAMBOURINES of various shapes are found among the wild Indians; only some of these are dealt with here.

The Iroquois drum, only about six inches in height and five in width, is like a small barrel with almost straight sides, and has a wooden hoop at each end. Over the upper end is stretched a piece of calfskin which is held fast by the hoop; the bottom is of wood, and the back oak drumstick is about seven-and-a-half inches long. The drum is used for the women's dance, the bird-dance and the various war-dances. In order to moisten the drumskin, some water is poured through a small hole low down at the side, which remains fully stopped up

---

c. Translation kindly supplied by W.R. Thomas and J.J.K. Rhodes of Burntisland, Scotland, who note that the literal meaning is 'several lignes' (sometimes spelt 'lines' or 'lynes'), the ligne being a twelfth of a Paris inch = 0.089 inches. d. Harrison (*Time, Place and Music*, p. 44) translates Torquemada's *contra bajo* as 'lower part'; for the original Spanish see ibid., p. 33.

while the drum is being played. The instrument which the writer examined gave the pitch of $a'$ [orig., 'small $a$'].

The drum of the Crees is shaped very much like a tambourine, and often has a diameter of over three feet, but is not very deep. The covering is made of the skin of a moose, with figures of people and animals crudely painted on it. A stick serves as beater (Franklin, chap. 3).

The Pueblo Indians make their drums from a hollow tree trunk, about two-and-a-half inches long and fifteen wide, with both ends covered by tanned hide; it is played with two beaters (Bancroft, vol. i, p. 552).

55     The Cherokees, Choctaws and Chickasaws used two drums in the form of earthen pots, over which was stretched a thin, dampened deerskin; the two musicians struck them noisily with beaters which were used, together with rattles, for accompanying songs at religious and warlike festivals (Adair).

The tambourine of the Twanas is wooden and square, one to two feet in length and breadth, with a depth of from three to five inches; it is covered with reindeer-skin, the leather braces of which cross underneath and are held by the left hand while the right hand beats on top. The pitch varies, according to the size of the instrument, between that of a small drum and a military drum.

The Assiniboines, Chippewas, Sioux and Montana Indians have similar tambourines, but they are round instead of square.

Rattles and clappers, likewise, are found in the most varied forms among all Indian tribes.

**b. Wind instruments.** The FLAGEOLET (Plate II, fig. 1) seems indigenous to all Indian tribes. It is made of cedar, sumach or elderwood; the last two are preferred because their pith is easy to remove. A branch or trunk with a diameter of one to one-and-a-quarter inches and a length of fifteen to twenty inches is selected. It is halved along its length and each half is hollowed out as far as B (see plate) and from B to A. The halves are then glued together and a quadrangular hole (C, D) is cut in the upper half on either side of B; four to eight soundholes are burnt into it. A wooden or metal plate (E) is placed over the square holes C and D so that its oblong rectangular shape notches into them exactly. A piece of wood (F), flat underneath and carved on top according to fancy, is fixed to the plate. A vibrating wooden or metal strip is often attached

56 to the incision in the plate. The pitch varies very much in different instruments; usually it resembles that of the D flute, except that the lowest note (with all fingerholes stopped) is often harsh and unpleasant. The principle of tone-production is the same as that in our ordinary small fife. The tuning is rarely pure; in most cases it includes the first four to six degrees of the major scale with their octaves (though this does not apply to every instrument). The flageolet is always used as a solo instrument, most frequently by young men who wish by this means to convey their love and tender feelings[85]. In order to entice the loved one to come out of her hut, the suitor plays a particular tune which is not played by anyone else. The flageolet is often decorated with colourful ribbons or leather thongs, crude paintings and suchlike.

The FLUTE (the flageolet is often erroneously called a flute) is less frequently found among the wild Indians. In fig. 2 of plate II is illustrated an Apache flute with three soundholes. The Pueblo Indians are said to accompany their dances and songs with flute-music; occasionally, it seems, even five or six players perform together on flutes of various sizes (Bancroft, vol. i, p. 552, footnote); further evidence on this point is lacking.

The PANPIPES (syrinx) are found among some wild Indian tribes in Mexico and Central America. This instrument reached a high level of perfection among the Peruvians (see Traill; also Garcilasso, as above).

57    Among many Pacific-Coast Indian tribes there exist double-reed pipes in which the reeds are bound together in the shape of the letter V (sometimes even three reeds are so bound) and these are blown with the mouth or nose (Bancroft).

Apart from these wind instruments there are also small pipes (war-pipes and the like); on the Pacific Coast are found instruments of wood which produce a rasping, earsplitting sound.

The Mexicans had wind instruments which were often mentioned, though only in passing, by the early Spanish historians. Among these were shawms *(zampoñas)*, crumhorns or cornetts *(cornetas)*, horns *(cuernos)*, coiled shells *(caracoles)*, and pipes *(chiflatos)*; many small pipes made of clay are still found. Nebel is of the opinion that they had only two pitches; one preserved in the Smithsonian Institute, however, gives the first five degrees of the major scale. The timbre is very like that of the Italian ocarina, as also is its shape. The remaining wind instruments are employed in both solo and ensemble playing; but their music would hardly be considered pleasant according to European concepts (Torquemada, vol. I, bk. II, chap. 88).

c. **Stringed instruments.**  These are not mentioned by any of the old writers (on the Mexicans), though the percussion and wind instruments were occasionally described in detail and frequently mentioned by them. Stringed instruments are hardly ever found among the wild Indians; the Apaches possess the one-stringed harpon[86] and are said to accompany their songs on it. Adair found a strange instrument of this variety, whose description must be given in his own words. He calls it 'one of their old sacred musical instruments. It pretty much resembled the Negroe-Banger (banjo) in shape, but far exceeded it in dimensions;

58   for it was about 5 feet long, and a foot wide at the head part of the board, with 8 strings made out of the sinews of a large buffalo. But they were so unskilful in acting the part of the Lyrick, that the Loache, or prophet, who held the instrument between his feet, and alongside of his chin, took one end of the bow, whilst a lusty fellow held the other; by sweating labor they scraped out such harsh jarring sounds, as might have been reasonably expected, by a soft ear, to have been sufficient to drive out the devil if he lay anywhere hid in the house'.

The Peruvians had the TINYA, a five-stringed instrument; three-stringed instruments have been seen among the Indians of the Orinoco valley.

# NOTES

1. The Seneca singer A-ō-doñ-wĕ made the following statement to the author: 'We have got the harvest-festival songs from Ha-we-ni-yu' (i.e. the Great Man above). The Mexicans had a similar myth (Clavigero, bk. VI, sect. 3). In Haïti a 'priest or legislator, Bohito III' introduced the music and the instruments (Rafinesque, vol. I, chap. VI, p. 191). In Yucatan and among the Dakotas the instruments allegedly came from the gods. On the origin and development of the arts among the savages, see Brown, sects. 3 and 4. Judging by the scanty and frequently contradictory reports that have come to us about the state of music among the Mexicans at the time of the Spanish conquest, it is not unlikely that the 'Consequences of the improvement in morals among the savages', as described by Brown (up to and including his sect. 31), bear the greatest resemblance to the progress of music and the related arts among the Aztec people. A scientific enquiry into this very interesting question would require the most detailed on-the-spot research; the writer of this paper has therefore made so bold as to offer only a few scattered, comparative observations on the subject. Up to the present, Brasseur de Bourbourg and Torquemada have done the most in this area.

2. The imitation of animals (especially of their body-movements) appears indeed very frequently to be connected with the songs, not however as an integrated part of them, but as a supplement to the scanty words. The music always appears to be an expression of human feeling, which is something totally different from an imitation of external nature. Words imitative of the most diverse natural sounds exist in almost all languages; but for joy (laughter), sadness and grief, man has his special organs of expression corresponding to his spiritual nature.

3. Baker's reference is faulty; the passage he quoted in translation occurs in Franklin's *Narrative of a journey to the shores of the Polar Sea* [see Bibliography]. It is not in chap, VIII of that volume (where indeed there is an account of the Dog-Ribs) but on p. 206, under date of July 1820. The dance was performed by Copper Indians, whose chief Akaitcho 'desired his young men to exhibit the Dog-Rib Indian dance'. The continuation is quoted here in Franklin's words.

4. Adair, pp. 97, 110, 164; Bancroft, Vol. I, pp. 704-5; Oviedo, pt. I, bk. V, chap. I; Torquemada, vol. II, bk. XIV, chap. XI; Catlin, vol. I, p. 368; Loskiel, p. 133; communicated in letters to the author from Y. Bonillas (Apaches) and Rev. E. Eels (Twanas, Clallams, etc.); this applies to almost all the Iroquois dances (A-ō-doñ-wĕ). It is possible that this round dance originally represented the course of the sun, since the Indians are sun-worshippers. This could equally be a basic reason for the universality of the round dance. The Indians at Milbank Sound (on the Pacific Coast, between 52 degrees and 56 degrees north) regard the sun as a shining man who travels round the earth while the latter remains still. They also have a performance in which the setting sun is represented by a splendidly-dressed chief (Dunn, pp. 171-2).

5. All writers are in agreement on this question.

6. See songs nos. X, XIX, XXVIII, XXIX, XXXII, XXXIX, XLII; Bancroft, vol. I, pp. 191, 281, 415; Dunn, pp. 225-6.

7. Torquemada, vol. II, bk. XIV, chap. XI; A-ō-doñ-wĕ had learnt the songs from his father; his small son had to rehearse them with the most painstaking care; see Rafinesque, vol. I, chap. VI.

8. Communicated in a letter to the author from Rev. Isaac Baird, Odanah, Wisconsin.

9. Torquemada; Oviedo, pt. I, bk. V, chap. I; the author got several Indians to sing examples of these 'new' songs which were very similar to the 'old' ones.

10. See especially Torquemada, bk. XVII, chap. III.

11. For information on the monthly festivals of the Mexicans see Torquemada, bk. XII, chap. XXXIV.

12. The 'Five Tribes': Senecas, Mohawks, Cayugas, Oneidas and Onondagas.

13. i.e. at public festivals.

14. A-ō-doñ-wĕ first answered the question 'Have these words any meaning?' with a firm 'No'; but after lively discussions back and forth with a friend, he was of the opinion that *wi-yo* meant (more or less) *good*; the meaning of *ka-noñ*, like most of the words used in the women's dance, was completely unknown to him. It may be that the meaning of the words of many old songs was forgotten by the Indians, or is known to a few initiates only (e.g., the medicine-men have a special cabbalistic language). Sahagun (vol. VII, p. 102) writes: '[There are] songs and psalms which are maintained unchanged, and which are sung although their meaning is no longer understood except by those who are born to and accustomed to that language'. See Brasseur de Bourbourg, *Quatre Lettres*, 2nd letter, section 5.

15. See Westphal, 'Rhythm', section 13: 'Earliest Origins of the Arts of the Muses'.

16. See songs nos. IV, V, VII.

17. No. XXXII (hi ye he!).

18. No. XXXIX, 19 (ha ya ha ya hi-hi-hi!). Civilized people have exactly the same exclamations.

19. No. XXXIX, 12.

20. See especially Adair; among the Cherokees and related tribes the sacred syllables were *Yo-he-wah* (Hebrew *Je-ho-va*); Adair constantly calls the Indians 'the red Hebrews' (pp. 97, 121, 164 etc.). The Hurons sang the same syllables (Heriot, pp. 82-3). The Nez-Percés used the syllables 'Ho-ha, ho-ha' in their songs for divine services (Dunn, pp. 225-6).

21. For the Mexicans see Brasseur, *Quatre Lettres*, 2nd letter, sect. 7; 4th letter, sect. 8 etc.; his explanation is at least very original and, like his opinions in general, of decided interest.

22. Mallery contains over two thousand such gestures.

23. Among many Indian tribes this had reached a not insignificant level of skill. See Brasseur, *Grammaire*, 'Ballet-Drame de Rabinal-Achi'; Clavigero, bk. VII, sect. 43; Acosta, bk. V, chap. XXIX; Bancroft, vol. I, pp. 170, 199, 393; Dunn, pp. 171-2; Loskiel, p. 133. The striking similarity of several performances has not escaped general notice. The use, at many festivals, of carved wooden masks seems to be general.

24. See Loskiel, p. 135; here the warrior sings of his Heroic Deeds and is accompanied by the others, as may be observed in no. IX.

25. Adair, p. 61.

26. See sect. 6.

27. This opinion is surprisingly corroborated in a report in the *Boston Herald* of 17th June 1881 on the research of Mr. F.H. Cushing among the Zuñis, where it is stated: 'In rhyme and rhythm the poetry is as perfect as the work of our most finished lyrists'.

28. This song, like the following one, has been taken from Powell.

29. Rafinesque, vol. I, chap. V. An English translation of these three historical songs can be found in the supplement to Brasseur's *Quatre Lettres*. The first and second songs, with copies of the Indian drawings, may be seen in Beach.

30. Name of a chief (noted by the writer).

31. The designation 'manly' is apparently used to mean 'courageous' or 'brave' for those who risked this dangerous passage; the Indian likes to praise his own deeds.

32. Oviedo, pt. I, bk. V, chap. I.

33. Cogolludo, bk. IV, chap. V, ap Landa.

34. Veytia, bk. III, chap. VII; Torquemada, bk. XII, chap. XXXIV; also bk. II, chap. XLI.

35. Brasseur; Bancroft.

36. As above.

37. For this situation among the Dakotas (Sioux) see Riggs, Introduction. See songs nos. XII to XVIII, in which the syllables 'ye! ye! ye!' are merely euphonious. (Communicated in a letter from Rev. T.L. Riggs.)

38. The Indians have never gone to the length of having a singing academy (in the European sense); the Spaniards found Mexican singing rough and unpleasant, although it later achieved excellence under Spanish direction (Torquemada, bk. XVII, chap. III).

39. Torquemada, bk. II, chap. LXXXVIII (Mexico); Oviedo, pt. I, bk. V, chap. I (Haïti); Bancroft, p. 281, footnote (Nez-Percés); communicated in letters to the writer from Rev. M. Eels (Twanas, Clallams, Chemakums), Rev. E. Vétromile (Micmacs etc.), Y. Bonillas (Apaches), Rev. Isaac Baird (Chippewas), Henry D. Wireman (Montana Indians); communicated orally to the writer from the Iroquois, Dakotas, Iowas, Kiowas, Poncas and Comanches.

40. Torquemada.

41. Three tribes who live not far from the Mexican border appear to be exceptions; they are the Pueblo Indians, the Apaches and the Comanches. The author does not know whether their accompaniment is really a harmonic one or whether they adopted it from the whites or the Aztecs.

42. Songs with a similar accompaniment on the tonic have also been heard among the Delawares and related tribes (Loskiel, p. 124), among the 'Socs and Sous' (communicated in a letter to the author from Dr. A.C. Garratt), as well as among the Twanas etc. (see M. Eels). This song (no. IX) was heard among the Mohawks already in the middle of the previous century (Mc Knight, pp. 77-9).

43. The essential elements in the melodic formulae will be discussed in detail in the next section.

44. See 'Table of Intervals'.

45. In the following examples the actual pitches are given; tunes in the key of G are sung one octave lower than notated.

46. No. X excepted, of course, since it is monotonal.

47. Paul, p. 15. These scales must be distinguished from the similarly-named transposition-scales of Aristoxenos, as well as from the sixteenth-century modes.

48. See the Chippewa war-song (no. XXXIII). It is worth mentioning that the Hindu scale 'sa' not only has the same tonal relationships, but also that it is

used in songs dealing with the subject of 'heroic love and valour'; see Jones. 'In the sixteenth century it was believed that this mode [the Ionian = ancient Lydian] was particularly suitable for creating a happy mood'. Paul, op. cit., p. 41.

49. Due to the superstition of the Indians, the author was prevented from including in his collection examples of the most commonly sung laments. The rare use of the minor third in the tunes transcribed below should not be regarded as typical of Indian songs in general (see nos. XXXIII to XLIII).

50. Paul, pp. 12-13.

51. *Die Lehre von der Harmonik;* a repetition of his ingenious and easily understood discussion would scarcely be in place here.

52. In these songs the plaintive tone was expressed chiefly by an appropriate manner of performance.

53. This is more like a dance-song; little lamenting was to be observed in the manner of its performance.

54. With the exception of recitative.

55. With the exception of monotonal tunes such as no. X.

56. The tonic is the chief momentary point of rest for the second.

57. This idea is based on examples such as nos. VII *c* 10, VIII *c* 3, XII *e* 6 from the end, XVIII *g* 13 etc.

58. On the question of the ending *(clausula)* Calvisius writes: 'This [intermediate] cadence occurs mainly on ending notes within the interval of a fifth, but most especially on the lowest note (that is, on the tonic), where also the final ending *(finis)* of a tune is established, and also on the highest note (therefore on the dominant) . . . and in the middle, where the fifth is divided into major and minor third'. [Quoted from the German of] Paul, op. cit., p. 41, 'Klarstellung der Tonarten des 16. Jahrhunderts', [who commented:] 'We could simply say that the triad supplied the notes for the ending'.

59. The only exception is mentioned below.

60. Judging by the character of the instruments and the dances generally.

61. As far as rhythmic development is concerned, the following suggestion is of course of a hypothetical nature; the correctness of the facts is vouched for by the author's own experience.

62. The beats (or the dancers' steps) are transcribed on the line above the staff. As in the case of the examples given above, one beat equals a quarter-note in simple time and a dotted quarter-note in compound time.

63. Many of these tunes give the impression that the metre was pulled, and thus drawn out of its regular rhythm.

64. The commonest metrical forms occurring among the Chippewas are 2/4 and 4/4 (communicated in a letter from Rev. I. Baird to the author), among the Pueblo Indians 2/4, 3/4 and 4/4 (letter from Rev. T.F. Ealy); among the Dakotas songs are mostly in 2/4, and in flute music in 3/4 (letter from Rev. A.L. Riggs), among the Micmacs 2/4, 4/4, 3/4 (letter from Rev. Eugene Vétromile); of twenty-four Twana songs, twenty are in binary measure (see no. XXXIX). In a collection of Negro songs from the former slave states, only six tunes out of one-hundred-and-thirty-six are in 3/4 metre as against eighty-three in 2/4, forty-five in 4/4 and two in 6/8. These tunes, unlike those of other collections, are not suitable for adapting to English stanzas, but are reproduced in their original form (Allen). As is well known, these Negro dances are remarkable more for their exact rhythm than for their gracefulness. In pre-Homeric times two- and three-beat metres existed among the Greeks.

65. *Elemente,* sect. 11.

66. *Archives,* vol. I, plate 52, and pp. 366 and 373.

67. *The Abnakis,* chap. VI.

68. Written communication to the writer, 10th December 1880.

69. Vol. I, chap. V; see also sect. 2.

70. A name for certain midnight orgies, or for those initiated into certain mysteries who are said to practice magic. A free translation of the word would be 'men of daybreak' (Schoolcraft).

71. Clavigero, bk. VII, pt. XLIV (with illustrations); Torquemada, bk. XIV, chap. XI.

72. Bancroft, vol. III, pp. 62-63. [Baker wrote 'vevtl' for Bancroft's 'vevetl'.]

73. Brasseur, *Grammaire,* p. 10.

74. ibid. (Ballet-drame de Rabinal-Achi).

75. ibid., *Essai,* p. 10.

76. Clavigero, (with illustrations).

77. Oviedo, pt. I, bk. V, chap. I.

78. Ibid.; Torquemada, bk. XIV, chap. XI; Nebel (with illustrations); on the other hand Brasseur (*Quatre Lettres,* 2nd letter, sect. 7, 'Observations') and

Clavigero state that only two parallel incisions were made (but if so how are there two different pitches?).

79. Nebel.

80. Ixtlilxóchitl, chap. LXVII.

81. Acosta, bk. VI, chap. XXVII; Oviedo, pt. I, bk. V, chap. I; Herrera, decade I, bk. III, chap. I, and others.

82. Brasseur. According to Bancroft (vol. I, p. 199) the Nootka (Columbia River) Indians have a type of drum made of a thick wooden plank which has been hollowed out from below; this is played with two beaters — perhaps an earlier form of the teponaztli?

83. *Events* [*recte: Incidents*] chap. VII.

84. Brasseur, op. cit. (see note 73); *Essai*, p. 9.

85. The Iroquois use the flageolet for this purpose although they have no love-songs; it was also used among the Peruvians; see Garcilasso, pt. I, bk. II, chap. XXVI. On the flageolet of the Mexicans, Nebel has written the following: 'The most complete instrument, and the one which leaves almost nothing to be desired, is their flageolet. Its range is that of a whole octave, but without the semitones, either because they did not recognise them or because they did not know how to play them. They were made of pottery' (with illustrations).

86. The Spanish name for the instrument (German *Harpune*), which is based on this characteristic form.

## Notenbeilagen.

Die ersten zweiunddreissig Lieder wurden vom Verfasser
eigenhändig notirt; in diesen Melodien ist der Schlag [vergl.
»Rhythmus«] einer Viertelnote (♩) bez. einer Viertelnote mit
Punkt (♩.) gleich; alle wurden von Männerstimmen, und die
meisten in hoher (baryton) Lage, gesungen; die hier notirte
Tonhöhe ist also eine Octave höher als die wirkliche.

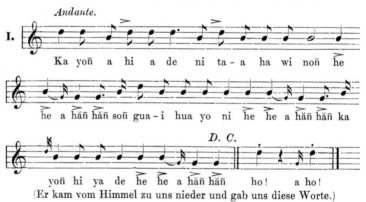

(Er kam vom Himmel zu uns nieder und gab uns diese Worte.)

Erstes Lied im Erntefest der Irokesen. Dieses Fest wird
alljährlich zur Zeit des Reifwerdens des Mais wiederholt; es
sind im ganzen 89 Lieder, die von zwei Sängern und stets in
derselben Ordnung gesungen werden; diese Aufführung dauert
3½ bis 4 Stunden mit einer längeren Pause und trägt einen
gottesdienstlichen Character. [Vergl. »Rhythmus« und auch
Loskiel, S. 133, »Tänze«].

# TRANSLATION OF GERMAN TEXT ACCOMPANYING THE
# NOTATED EXAMPLES

The first thirty-two songs were transcribed by the author personally; the beat in these tunes (see sect. 6) is equivalent to a crotchet ( ♩ ) or a dotted crotchet ( ♩. ); all were sung by men and mostly in the upper (baritone) register; the pitch notated here is therefore an octave higher than the actual pitch.

I       He came down to us from heaven and gave us these words.

This is the first of the Iroquois harvest-festival songs. The festival takes place every year when the maize is ripe. There are eighty-nine songs altogether, which are sung by two singers, always in the same order. The performance lasts three-and-a-half to four hours, including a long interval, and it has the character of a divine service. (See sect. 6 and also Loskiel, p. 133, 'Dances'.)

## 60

Yo soñ gua we ni yo hăñ-ăñ yo ho ho
ho hăñ-ăñ yo hăñ-ăñ! yo hăñ-ăñ hăñ-ăñ soñ gua
we ni yo soñ gua we ni hăñ yo! h'yo!

(Uebersetzung fehlt.)

**Viertes Lied im Erntefest.**

To ta yo nĭ-i! ye ta ke noñ ge yo ho ho
ho! ho ho ho ho! ho! ho! to ta yo ni ye ta ye
ta ye noñ ge yo năñ ni yo! o - o!

To-ta-yo-ni ye-ta-ke-noñ-ge
Wolf rennt.

**Fünftes Lied im Erntefest.**

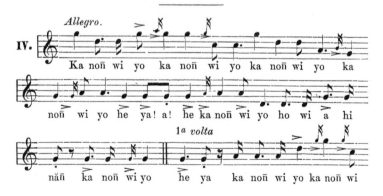

Ka noñ wi yo ka noñ wi yo ka noñ wi yo ka
noñ wi yo he ya! a! he ka noñ wi yo ho wi a hi
năñ ka noñ wi yo he ya ka noñ wi yo ka noñ wi

II       Translation is missing.

This is the fourth harvest-festival song.

III     To-ta-yo-ni                ye-ta-ke-noñ-ge

           Wolf                       runs

The fifth harvest-festival song.

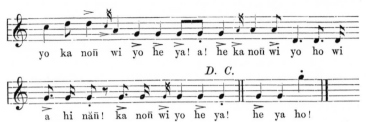

yo ka noñ wi yo he ya! a! he ka noñ wi yo ho wi

*D. C.*

a hi näñ! ka noñ wi yo he ya! he ya ho!

(In diesem Lied, sowie in allen Liedern des »Weibertanzes«, sollen
die Wörter keine besondere Bedeutung haben.)

Ein Lied im »Weibertanze« der Irokesen; nur Weiber tanzen; die Lieder werden ohne bestimmte Ordnung von einem
Chor junger Männer gesungen; diese sitzen im Tanzsaale und
begleiten ihren Gesang mit rhythmischen Schlägen. In diesem
Falle waren 17 Sänger zugegen; 15 hatten keine Ratteln und
zwei schlugen auf Pauken; die Schläge wurden unisono ausgeführt.

---

*Allegro.*

**V.**

Ka noñ wi yo ya ne ka noñ wi yo noñ he

ya ka noñ he ya noñ he ya he ya! ka noñ wi

yo he ya he ho he yo no he ya he ya

1ª *volta*          *D. C.* 2ª *volta*

ho he ya no he ya he ya! ya no he ya

he ya ho he ya - a ho.

Ein Lied im Weibertanze der Irokesen.

---

IV       In this song, as in all songs for the women's dance, the words appear to have no special meaning.

This song is for the Iroquois women's dance, which is danced only by women. The songs are sung by a choir of young men, and not in any pre-determined order. They sit in the dance-hall and accompany their singing by beating rhythmically. In this particular instance there were seventeen singers present, fifteen of whom had small rattles while two beat on drums. The beats were played in unison.

V  A song for the Iroquois women's dance.

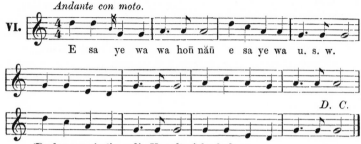

## 62

**VI.** *Andante con moto.*

E sa ye wa wa hoñ nǎñ e sa ye wa u. s. w.

*D. C.*

(Du kannst sie [i. e. die Kugel] nicht finden.)

Beim Hazardspiel unter den Indianern wird eine Kugel in einen von vier Moccasins (Indianerschuhe) geworfen, um welche die Spieler im Kreise sitzen; die Kugel geht geschwind von einem zum andern, und dieses Lied wird gesungen, um die Aufmerksamkeit desjenigen Spielers, der zu errathen hat, wo die Kugel endlich versteckt wird, abzulenken.

---

**VII.** *Allegro.*

Yu a he - e he ya! yu a he he a ha!

kan i wa sa se a he ya! wi a - a yo ha he - e

*1a volta D. C. 2a volta*

noñ! kan i wa sa se a he ya! ya! he ya!

(Die Wörter haben keine Bedeutung.)

Kriegslied der Irokesen.

---

**VIII.** *Allegro moderato.*

We yo hi yo we hi ǎñ we yo hi yo we hi ǎñ

VI        You cannot find it (i.e. the bullet).

In an Indian game of chance a bullet is thrown into one of four moccasins
(Indian shoes) around which the players sit in a circle. The bullet passes quickly
from one to the next, and this song is sung in order to distract the attention of
the player, who has to guess, from where the bullet is finally concealed.

VII       The words have no meaning.

An Iroquois war-song.

we yo hi yo we hi ăn̄ hi ya hi ya ho ho nod di ho

*D. C.*

ya wi ho-o we hi ăn̄ hui ă! ă! hui ĕ! ĕ!

yo! h' yo! h' yo!

(Die Wörter haben keine Bedeutung.)

Kriegslied der Irokesen.

———

*Andante con moto.*

**IX.** I ge i ge i ge hon ni hĕ! i ge

Yĕ! yĕ! yĕ! u. s. w.

hon ni hĕ! i ge i ge i ge hon ni hĕ! u. s. w.

(Ich gehe! ich gehe!)

Kriegslied der Irokesen (vergl. »Poesie«).

———

*Andante con moto.*        *5 volte* D. C.

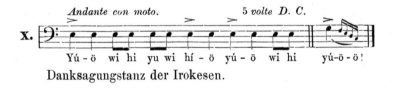

**X.** Yú - ö wi hi yu wi hí - ö yú - ö wi hi yú-ö-ö!

Danksagungstanz der Irokesen.

———

VIII    The words have no meaning.

An Iroquois war-song.

IX     I go! I go!

Iroquois war-song (see sect. 2).

X Iroquois thanksgiving song.

## 64

*Allegro.*

**XI.**

O la ko ta ku wa ki ya pe! o la
ko ta ku wa ki ya pe! o la ko ta
ku wa ki ya pe! o la ko ta ku wa
ki ya pe lo he - e o! Shung ma ni
tu sa pa a ki ci ta o ma ni ye lo!
o la ko ta ku wa ki ya pe! o la ko
ta ku wa ki ya pe o pe - e o!

| O-lá-ko-ta | kú-wa kí-ya-pe | Shung-má-ni-tu | sá-pa |
|---|---|---|---|
| Friede | kommt man sagt | Wolf | schwarz |
| A-kí-ci-ta | o-má-ni | | ye-lo |
| Krieger | geht | | [emphatisch]. |

Der »Omahatanz«, Lieblingstanz verschiedener Indianernationen (von den Dakotas oder Sioux).

*Andante con moto.*

**XII.**

Shi ce shi ce shan te ma shi cä shi
ce la ka shi ce na pi ma yu zä - - - ä!

XI   O-lá-ko-ta      kú-wa ki-ya-pe   Shung-má-ni-tu   sá-pa

Joy            comes one says      Wolf        black

A-ki-ci-ta      o-má-ni      ye-lo

Warrior        goes      (emphatic)

The Omaha dance, a lovers' dance performed by various Indian tribes (of the Dakota or Sioux).

ä - - ä shi ce wan ci ya ke shni shi

ce shan te ma shi cä shi ce la ka shi ce na

pe ma yu zä - - ä!

(Shi-cé shi-cé shan-té ma-shí-cä
Schwager, Schwager, Herz mein - schlecht
Shi-cé-la ka shi-cé na-pé ma-yú-zä
Lieber Schwager Schwager Hand meine - nimm
Shi-cé wañ - cí — ya-ke — shni
Schwager seh' ich — dich — nicht
Shi-cé shan-té ma - shí - cä
Schwager Herz mein - schlecht
Shi-cé-la ka shi-cé na-pé ma-yú-zä
Lieber Schwager Schwager Hand meine - nimm.)

Dakota »Nachtgesang«; Serenade, oder Ständchen; wird von mehreren jungen Männern, die mit einer Pauke durch das Dorf oder Lager ziehen, gesungen.

*Molto allegro.*

**XIII.**

Wa ya ka wan wa ni kte lo e ha yun kan oñ si

la ka ma hin gle-e wa rte shni kin i ra ma ya

ye ye e ya yo he yo!

(Wa-ya-ka wan
Gefangener ein [kommt]
Wa-ni kte lo e - ha
»Ich leben will« ihr sagt
Yun-kan oñ-si-la-ka ma-hin-gle
Und so Mitleid kommt über mich
Wa-rte-shni kin i-ra-ma-ya
Elende der macht mich lustig.)

Scalptanz der Dakotas.

5

XII       Shi-cé         shi-cé       shan-té   ma-shí-cä

Brother-in-law, brother-in-law  heart    my  bad

        Shi-cé-la       ka      shi-cé     na-pé   ma-yú-zä

Dear brother-in-law      brother-in-law hand   my  take

        Shi-cé     wañ-cí   —   ya-ke   —   shni

Brother-in-law  see  I       you       not

        Shi-cé     shan-té   ma-shí-cä

Brother-in-law  heart    my  bad

        Shi-cé-la       ka      shi-cé     na-pé   ma-yú-zä

Dear brother-in-law      brother-in-law hand   my  take.

Dakota night-song, a serenade sung by several young men who march with a drum through the village or camp.

XIII     Wa-ya-ka        wan

       Prisoner (comes)  in

       Wa-ni  kte  lo   e-ha

       'I want to live', you say

       Yun-kan oñ-si-la-ka ma-hin-gle

       And so pity overcomes me

       Wa-rte-shni kin i-ra-ma-ya

         Misery which makes me joyous

A Dakota scalp-dance.

113

## 66

*Allegro.*

**XIV.**

Ko la ta ku ya ka pe lo - o o ki ci ze

i ma tan can ye lo - o e ha ka lesh le ħaǹ wa oǹ

we lo e ye ye ye lo!

(Ko-la ta-ku ya-ka-pe lo
Freund etwas ihr meint
O-ki-ci-ze i-ma-tan-can ye-lo e-ha ka-lesh
»[Im] Kampfe ich bin Führer« ihr sagt
Le-ħaǹ wa-oǹ we-lo
Nun ich bin). Oder: —
(Freund, ihr meint etwas;
Ihr sagt: »ich bin ein grosser Streiter«;
Nun, ich bin auch da!)

### Scalptanz der Dakotas.

*Allegro.*

**XV.**

Maħ pi ya mi me me ya - a kli na jin pe lo maħ pi ya

mi me me ya - a kli na jin pe lo! ko la ni hin ci ya

pe wan yan ki ye - e! ye ye ye yo!

(Maħ-pí-ya mi-mé-me-ya gli-ná-jin-pe lo
Wolken runde (rollende) ziehen zusammen
Ko-lá ni-hiń-ci-ya-pe wan-ya-ka
Freund [die] Eilenden [Erschrockenen] seht.) Oder:
(Rollende Wolken steigen
Freund, sieh wie sie vorübereilen.)

### Dakota Lied.

XIV     Ko-la    ta-ku    ya-ka-pe lo

     Friend something you believe

     O-ki-ci-ze i-ma-tan-can     ye-lo e-ha ka-lesh

     '(In) battle I am leader',      you say

     Le-ħañ wa-oñ we-lo

     Now    I am.

          or:

> Friend, you believe something;
> You say: 'I am a great champion';
> Now, I am also here!

Dakota scalp-dance.

XV     Ma-pi-ya mi-mé-me-ya    gli-ná-jin-pe   lo

     Clouds    round (rolling) draw together

     Ko-lá   ni-hiń-ci-ya-pe      wan-ya-ka

     Friend (who terrified) islands sees

          or:

> Rolling clouds mount;
> Friend, see how they hurry by.

Dakota song.

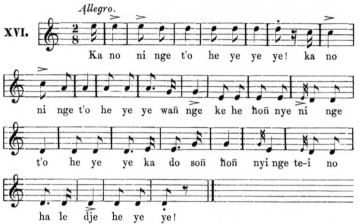

## 67

**XVI.**

Ka no ni nge t'o he ye ye ye! ka no
ni nge t'o he ye ye wañ nge ke he ñoñ nye ni nge
t'o he ye ye ka do soñ ñoñ nyi nge te-i no
ha le dje he ye ye!

(Unser Führer ist hin; wo aber sind die Dakotas? Sie sind getödtet!)
Iowa [aï-o-wa] Kriegslied; feiert einen über die Dakotas
gewonnenen Sieg.

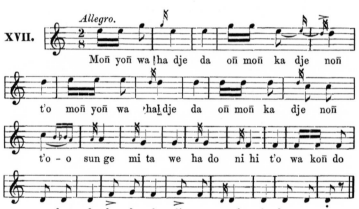

**XVII.**

Moñ yoñ wa ha dje da oñ moñ ka dje noñ
t'o moñ yoñ wa hal dje da oñ moñ ka dje noñ
t'o-o sun ge mi ta we ha do ni hi t'o wa koñ do
wa hoñ do he do ska éi we noñ ha t'o he ye ye!

(Wenn ich in die Schlacht gehe, hab' ich keine Furcht; hilf mir, o
Gott! richte deine Blicke auf mein Pferd und schlage den Feind nieder.)

Gesang eines iowa Kriegers, der mit einem schlechten
Pferd in die Schlacht muss.

5*

XVI    Our leader is away; but where are the Dakotas? They have been killed!

Iowa (aí-o-wa) war song, commemorating a victory over the Dakotas.

XVII    When I go into battle, I have no fear; help me, O God! direct your gaze at my horse and strike down my enemy.

Song of an Iowa warrior who must go to battle on an inadequate horse.

## 68

**XVIII.** *Allegretto.*

Hing ge wo ha ba ke ye ye ye hing

ge wo ha ba ke ye ye ye tañ wa ya

de ye ye nañ dje ye gua he ye dje ka wa oñ

noñ hi noñ go tañ wa de noñ dje - e gua hăñ găñ

wa - a ha ba ke ye ye ye tañ wa de - i

năñ dje - e gua ye ye ye ye ye ye!

Iowa Liebeslied; wird von den jungen Kriegern beim Ausreiten gesungen.

**XIX.** *Allegretto.*

Yo ha ni ne yo ha ni ne yo ha ni ne

yo ha ni ne he é - i yo ha ni ne hi ya!

Iowa »Bohnentanz«; ein gottesdienstliches oder Danksagungsfest.

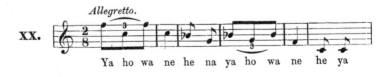

**XX.** *Allegretto.*

Ya ho wa ne he na ya ho wa ne he ya

XVIII    Iowa love-song, sung by young warriors when out riding.

XIX    Iowa bean-dance for a religious or thanksgiving festival.

119

ha ni he  ho wa  ne  he na  ya ho wa  ne - e  he  na  u. s. w.

**Iowa »Bohnentanz«.**

---

*Allegro.*

**XXI.**

Wi he ye ha wi he ye ha hi  ya he he

wi hi wi  hi ye ha  hi  i  ye hi ye  pa ni

ḣoñ nye wa ta goñ da ci  oñ gi we ḣi gi do ke

ya hăñ ha ye  wi ye ha he he ye hi [ye - e!

**Iowa Siegeslied; Sieg über die Pawnees [»pa-ni«].**

---

*Allegro.*

**XXII.**

Dja de wi dje ha ke i he  g'a dja de wi dje ha

ke i he  g'a wa coñ  ta yăñ  i  dje ha ke dja

de wi dje ha  ke i  he  g'a.

**Iowa »Weibertanz«; Danksagungsfest.**

---

XX      Iowa bean-dance.

XXI     Iowa song of victory, commemorating a victory over the Pawnees ('pa-ni').

XXII    Iowa women's dance for a thanksgiving festival.

## 70

XXIII.

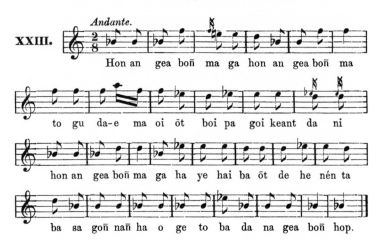

Hon an gea boñ ma ga hon an gea boñ ma
to gu da-e ma oi ōt boi pa goi keant da ni
hon an gea boñ ma ga ha ye hai ba ōt de he nén ta
ba sa goñ nañ ha o ge to ba da na gea boñ hop.

(Ich hab' ihn lange nicht gesehen; viel junge Männer giebts, ich aber liebe den Einen, meinen Sohn; wenn er zurückkommt, werde ich ihn sehen; ich wache jede Nacht, bis er kommt; er wird sich freuen, mich zu sehen.)

## Kiowa Lied der Mutter an den abwesenden Sohn.

XXIV.

Ga de ōt sa - a goñ a pe ta pe k'o a
ka be de ōt sa - a goñ ya keañ poñ ma koi ga
de ōt sa - a goñ iadl keañ da hoñ em boñ ma ba oñ dep.

(Ich weine auf dem Berge sitzend; ich weine bis es Nacht wird; weil ich mein Mädchen sehen will, deswegen wein' ich; aber ich hoffe nach einigen Monaten in die Heimath zu gehen und die Geliebte zu sehen.)

## Kiowa Liebeslied.

XXIII    I have not seen him for a long time; there are many young men, but I love one, my son. When he comes back I shall see him; I lie awake every night until he comes; he will rejoice when he sees me again.

Kiowa song of a mother to her absent son.

XXIV    I weep while sitting on the mountain; I weep until it is night; because I want to see my sweetheart, for that reason I weep; but I hope in a few months to return to my country and see my love.

Kiowa love-song.

## 71

**XXV.**

*Allegro molto.*

Ho wa he yas te - e ho - o na yo o i nui

ka i ho yo ri shi vi tañ no he he ye ye he ye he ye - e

he ye he ye ye ye ye ye ye.

(Freunde — Stein — bleiben immer fest — vorwärts!)

Kriegslied der Cheyennes.)

---

**XXVI.**

*Allegro molto.*

u. s. w.

Kriegslied der Cheyennes.

---

**XXVII.**

*Andante con moto.*

Ka de le wats ta wa ta wi ka na ni wi ca ta

ki wi ko la wi kéts o ha di we li tsa ka sa.

(Grosser Büffel [Häuptling] ging in den Krieg und kam nicht zurück; wir trauern deshalb und möchten ihn sehen.)

Pawnee Kriegslied. [?]

XXV    Friends — stone — always remain firm — forward!

Cheyenne war-song.

XXVI    Cheyenne war-song

XXVII    Great Buffalo (chief) went into battle and did not return; thus we are sad and wish to see him.

Pawnee war-song (?)

## 72

XXVIII.

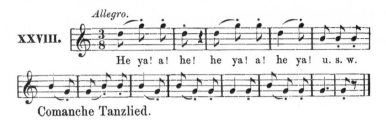

He ya! a! he! he ya! a! he ya! u. s. w.

Comanche Tanzlied.

XXIX.

Hi ye ho hi ye ho u. s. w.

Comanche Tanzlied.

XXX.

No-o da- añ la g'li dañ t'eoñ la g'li de

no dañ la g'li da- añ t'eoñ la g'li dañ no yo dañ

la g'li dañ t'eon la g'li de e na ne te di wa kañ da-e

we ka tañ he wa ka dañ e ha tañ we

Ponca Liebeslied.

## 73

*Allegro.*

XXXI.

A ki le li wañ pe a ki le li wañ pe
a ki le li wañ pe a ki le li wañ pe he ye
hi di ku la shañ ge we go la she lo a ki le
li wañ pe - e ye!

Ponca Kriegslied.

*Allegro.*

XXXII.

Hi ye he ye-e he ye he ye he ye u. s. w.

Ponca »Sonnentanz«.

XXXIII.

Kriegslied der Chippewas. [Aus Schoolcraft's Archives of
Aborginal Knowledge, vol. V.]

XXXI    Ponca war-song

XXXII   Ponca sun-dance.

XXXIII  Chippewa war-song. (From Schoolcraft, vol. V).

## 74

XXXIV.

Wŏ wŏ te si wŏ wŏ te si i mau i shin

ci bwŏ ni bō ni wi bi i gŏn bi i

gŏn i wi wŏ wŏ te si wŏ wŏ te si

was sa kun ēn dji gŏn.

(Kleines weisses fliegendes Licht, leuchte mir beim Schlafengehen, lass' mich deine kleine weisse Flamme in meiner Nähe sehen; kleines weisses fliegendes Licht, zeig' mir deine helle Fackel.)

Chippewa Kinderlied an die Feuerfliege [1]) [Herr Prof. T. W. Chittenden, Appleton, Wis., war so freundlich die von ihm gesammelten Indianerlieder (XXXIV bis incl. XXXVIII) dem Verf. zu schicken].

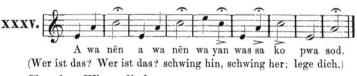

XXXV.

A wa nēn a wa nēn wa yan was sa ko pwa sod.

(Wer ist das? Wer ist das? schwing hin, schwing her; lege dich.)

Cherokee Wiegenlied.

XXXVI.

Muscogee [?] Trauergesang.

---

1) Der Sprung von der grossen Septime zur kleinen Sext, so merkwürdig er auch erscheinen mag, soll in der modernen Musik der Hindus nicht selten vorkommen; (vgl. Tagore, Engl. Verses set to Hindu Music, Calcutta, 1875, pp. 83, 105 u. s. w.).

XXXIV  Little white flying light, shine on me as I go to sleep; let me see your little white flame near me; little white flying light, show me your bright flare.

Chippewa children's song to the firefly. (Professor T.W. Chittenden of Appleton, Wisconsin, was so kind as to send the writer Indian songs that he had collected — nos. XXXIV to XXXVIII.) The leap of the major seventh to the minor sixth, remarkable as it may seem, occurs not infrequently in modern Hindu music (see Tagore, pp. 83, 105, etc.). [Baker noted in his *errata* that the first note of this tune should be $d'$.]

XXXV  Who is that? Who is that? Swing backwards, swing forwards, lie down.

Cherokee lullaby.

XXXVI  Muscogee (?) lament.

## 75

Lied der Brotherton-Indianer.

Der Sage zufolge wurde dieses Lied von den an der atlan-
tischen Küste wohnenden Völkern einige Jahre vor Ankunft
der Weissen gehört, als käme es vom Himmel; man hielt es
für Geistermusik und brauchte es nur zu hohen Festen.

No. 1. Bootgesang.

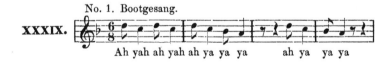

Ah yah ah yah ah ya ya ya    ah ya    ya ya

XXXVII   Song of the Brotherton Indians.

XXXVIII According to the legend this song was heard, as though it came from heaven, by people living on the Atlantic coast some years before the arrival of the whites; it was regarded as music of the spirits and was used only at important festivals.

## 76

No. 2. Bootgesang.

ah ya ya ya     ya ya   ya ya ya ya.

No. 3. Spielgesang.

Hin ni hai ni

No. 4.          No. 5. Spielgesang.

hai hai ni.     Hi ha hi.     Hwi a ho.

No. 6. Spielgesang.          No. 7. Spielgesang.

Ha  ha ha etc.               He ye ha la la.

No. 8. Spielgesang.

No. 9. Spielgesang.          No. 10. Kind.

Ta-ka-tas skulle-e.

No. 11. Trauer.          No. 12. Trauer.

Oh d-da   d-da  d-da.

No. 13. Krieg.

Ho-ya-chi-chis,   ho-ya-chi-chis,   etc.

No. 14. Wind.          Bass zu 14.

Hi - i  hi-i   hi - i.

No. 15. Krank.

XXXIX   [The song-titles are given here as they appear in Eels]
No. 1, Boat Song; no. 2, Boat Song; no. 3, Gambling Song; nos. 5 to 9, Gambling Songs; no. 10, Baby; no. 11, Mourning; no. 12, Mourning; no. 13, War; no. 14, Wind, [followed by] Base for 14; nos. 15 to 17, Sick; nos. 18 to 20, Dance; nos. 21 to 24, Black Tamano-us.

## 77

No. 16. Krank.  No. 17. Krank.

Hi - i - e  hi - i - e  hi - e.   He - he - e - a  he - e - a

No. 18. Tanz.

he - e - a, etc.   Hu - ni - a - wa - hi - hit.

No. 19. Tanz.   No. 20. Tanz.

Ha - ya ha-ya-hi-hi-hi.

No. 21. Schwarzer Tamano-us.   No. 22. Schwarzer Tamano-us.

Ho - ho -hoy ho-hoy.   Ha - ha - hoy  hwi - hi - hi.

No. 23. Schw. Tamano-us.   No. 24. Schw. Tamano-us.

Ha - hoy-hu-hi-ni.

Gesänge der Twanas, Clallams und Chemakums; [aus
The Amer. Antiquarian für April, Mai und Juni 1879; notirt
vom Rev. M. Eells, Skokomish, Washington Territory].

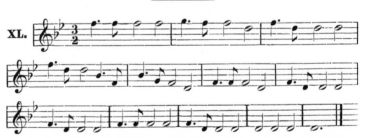

XL.

Chippewa Scalptanz. [Dieses Lied, sowie das nächstfolgende, sind Keating's Exploration to the Source of the St.
Peter's River, vol. 1., entnommen].

Songs of the Twanas, Clallams, and Chemakums (notated by M. Eels, Skokomish, Washington Territory).

XL     Chippewa scalp-dance. (This song, and the following one, have been taken from Keating, vol. I.)

## 78

XLI.

Sioux »Hundetanz«.

XLII.

1.
Hi tu e oo ha ha hi tu e oo ha ha ha ha ha ha ha ha ha ha

2.
Hi tu e - a tut-t – t - tut-t - tut-t - t - t - tut

3.
Wa – a ich e - e wa - - a

ich e - e Wa-a ich Wa-a ich.

Lieder der Walla-walla Indianer. 1 und 2 wurden von einer alten Frau in gewissen zauberärztlichen Ceremonien gesungen. Männer und Knaben begleiteten die Gesänge mit rhythmischen Schlägen und auch mit der Stimme. 3 wurde beim Hazardspiel gesungen.

[Aus Wilke's Exploring Expedition, vol. IV, p. 400.]

XLI    Sioux dog-dance.

XLII    Songs of the Walla-walla Indians. Nos. 1 and 2 were sung by an old woman at certain magic ceremonies. Men and boys accompanied the songs vocally and also by beating rhythmically. No. 3 was sung while playing a game of chance. (From Wilkes, vol. IV, p. 400). [Baker has incorrectly copied the second staff; the note *a'* should be a quarter-note.]

## 79

## XLIII.

**1.**

Shi ce ta ku ya kan ak he i ye ni tan shi wa ya shi ce

ce shi ce ta ku ya kan a kan he.

**2.**

Hor bo ju hok shi na kin ta ku e ya pi

wi ca ka pi shni tu ka a te ka o ma ki ya

a te ca o ma ki ya ca i to i yuk can we.

**3.**

He nan jin we he nan jin we-e u kta ce u kta ke

ya ca! wa mdi da ta u kta ce u kta ke ya ca!

(Halt da, sag' ich! halt da, sag' ich! kommen wird er, er will kommen, er sagte es; Rother Adler, er wird kommen, er kommt, er sagte es.)

**4.**

Tu wesh he ce cash ko ki pa ko ki pe dan ka-a! tu

wesh he ce cash ko ki pa ko ki pe dan ka-a!

(Wer hätte vor so einem Menschen Furcht,
Sich fürchten, wahrhaftig!
Wer hätte vor so einem Menschen Furcht,
Sich fürchten, wahrhaftig!)

XLIII    no. 3. Stop there, I say! stop there, I say! come he will, he will come, he said so; Red Noble One, he will come, he comes, he said so.

        no. 4. Who would have feared such a human fear, truly!
                Who would have feared such a human fear, truly!

## 80

Vier Liebeslieder der Dakotas; 1. und 2. sind von Herrn R. H. Hamilton, Hampton, Va., im Auftrage des Verf. notirt worden; die beiden anderen (sowie die Uebersetzungen zu XII, XIII. XIV und XV) hat ihm Rev. T. L. Riggs, Fort Sully, Dakota Territory freundlichst übersandt.

———————

Four Dakota love-songs. Nos. 1 and 2 were transcribed by Mr. R.H. Hamilton, Hampton, Vancouver, at the request of the author; the two others, and also the translations of nos. XII, XIII, XIV and XV, were most kindly sent to him by Rev. T.L. Riggs, Fort Sully, Dakota Territory.

# Tabelle der Tonstufen.

XVIII. (5—5).
5 6 1 2 3 4 5 6 1

XIX. (1—5).
5 6 1 2 4

XX. (1—?).
5 1 2 4 5 1

XXI. (5—1).
6 1 2 3 4 5

XXII. (5—5).
5 6 1 2 3 5

XXIII. (1—1).
1 3 4 #4 5 7

XXIV. (1—1).
1 3 5

XXV. (1—5).
5 1 2 3

XXVI. (2—?).
4 5 1 2 3 5 1 2

XXVII. 1—1).
5 6 1 2

XXVIII. (5—1),
1 3 5 1

XXIX. (3—6).
5 6 1 2 3 5 6 1 2 3

XXX. (1—5).
5 6 1 2 3 4 5 6 1 2

XXXI. (3—1).
1 2 4 5 1 2 3

XXXII. (1—1).
6 1 2 4 5 6 1 2

6

145

Table of Intervals and Metre

# Tabellen der Intervalle und des Tacts.

| Intervals | Intervalle. | | | | | | | Tact. | | | | Metre |
|---|---|---|---|---|---|---|---|---|---|---|---|---|
| I | 1 | | 3 | | 5 | | | Unregelmässig | | | | Irregular |
| II | 1 | 2 | ♭3 | | 5 | | ♭7 | | ²/₄ | | | |
| III | 1 | 2 | ♭3 | 4 | 5 | | | | ²/₄ | | | |
| IV | 1 | 2 | 3 | 4 | 5 | | | Unregelmässig | | | | Irregular |
| V | 1 | 2 | 3 | 4 | 5 | 6 | ♭7 | | ²/₄ | | | |
| VI | 1 | 2 | 3 | 4 | 5 | 6 | | | | ⁴/₄ | | |
| VII | 1 | 2 | 3 | 4 | 5 | 6 | 7 | | | | ³/₈ | |
| VIII | 1 | 2 | 3 | 4 | 5 | 6 | | | | ⁴/₄ | | |
| IX | 1 | 2 | | 4 | 5 | | | ²/₈ | | | | |
| X | 1 | | | | | | | Unregelmässig | | | | Irregular |
| XI | 1 | 2 | 3 | 4 | 5 | | | | ²/₄ | | | |
| XII | 1 | 2 | 3 | | 5 | 6 | | | | | ³/₈ | |
| XIII | 1 | 2 | 3 | 4 | 5 | 6 | | | ²/₄ | | | |
| XIV¹⁾ | 1 | | ♭3 | 4 | 5 | | ♭7 | ²/₈ | | | | |
| XV | 1 | 2 | 3 | 4 | 5 | 6 | ♭7 | | ²/₄ | | | |
| XVI | 1 | 2 | | 4 | 5 | | ♭7 | ²/₈ | | | | |
| XVII | 1 | 2 | ♭3 | 4 | 5 | | ♭7 | ⁴/₁₆ | | | | |
| XVIII | 1 | 2 | 3 | 4 | 5 | 6 | | | | | ³/₈ | |
| XIX | 1 | 2 | | 4 | 5 | 6 | | | ²/₄ | | | |
| XX | 1 | 2 | | 4 | 5 | | | ²/₈ | | | | |
| XXI | 1 | 2 | 3 | 4 | 5 | 6 | | | | | ³/₈ | |
| XXII | 1 | 2 | 3 | | 5 | 6 | | | ²/₄ | | | |
| XXIII²⁾ | 1 | | 3 | 4 | 5 | | 7 | ²/₈ | | | | |
| XXIV | 1 | | 3 | | 5 | | | ²/₈ | | | | |
| XXV | 1 | 2 | 3 | | 5 | | | | ²/₄ | | | |
| XXVI | 1 | 2 | 3 | 4 | 5 | | | | ²/₄ | | | |
| XXVII | 1 | 2 | | | 5 | 6 | | | ²/₄ | | | |
| XXVIII | 1 | | 3 | | 5 | | | | | | ³/₈ | |
| XXIX | 1 | 2 | 3 | | 5 | 6 | | | ²/₄ | | | |
| XXX | 1 | 2 | 3 | 4 | 5 | 6 | | | ²/₄ | | | |
| XXXI | 1 | 2 | 3 | 4 | 5 | | | | ²/₄ | | | |
| XXXII | 1 | 2 | | 4 | 5 | 6 | | | ²/₄ | | | |
| | 32 | 26 | 25³⁾ | 22 | 31 | 15 | 8⁴⁾ | 7 | 15 | 2 | 5 | |

1) XIV hat auch grosse Septime. — 2) XXIII hat auch übermässige Quarte. — 3) Vier Melodien haben kleine, 21 grosse Terz. — 4) Sechs Melodien haben kleine, zwei haben grosse Septime, und eine hat beide.

1) No. XIV has also a major seventh. 2) No. XXIII has also an augmented fourth. 3) Four tunes have minor thirds, twenty-one have major. 4) Six tunes have minor sevenths, two have major, and one has both.

146

Tafel I.

147

# Tafel II.

Fig. I.

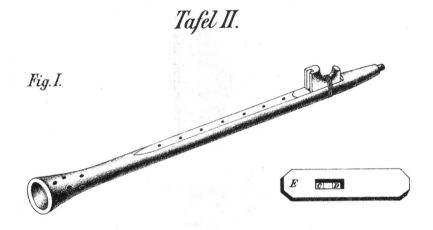

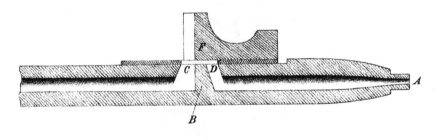

Fig. II.

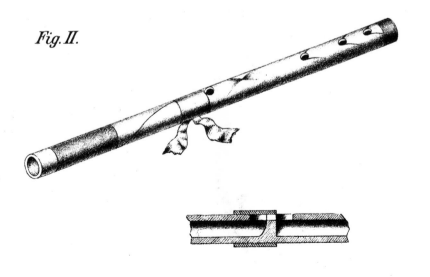

# LIST OF WORKS CITED BY BAKER

Some are given in more recent editions (and original language, if English) where these are known to exist.

Acosta, José de, *Historia natural y moral de las Indias,* Seville 1590; ed. F. Mateos, Madrid 1954, ed. E. O'Gorman. Mexico 1962.

Adair, James, *The History of the American Indians,* London 1775; ed. Samuel Cole Williams, Johnson City (Tenn) 1930, reprinted 1953.

Allen, William F. and others, *Slave Songs of the United States,* New York 1867.

Bancroft, H.H., *The native races of the Pacific States,* 5 vols., New York, 1874; Leipzig, 1875.

Beach, W.W., ed., *The Indian Miscellany; containing papers on the history, antiquities, arts, languages, religions, traditions and superstitions of the American aborigines,* Albany 1877.

Brasseur de Bourbourg, *Collection de documents dans les langues indigènes,* 4 vols., Paris 1861-1868. Vol. II was *Gramatica de la Lengua Quiché . . . suivi d'un essai sur la poésie, la musique, la danse et l'art dramatique chez les Mexicains et les Guatémaltèques avant la conquête,* 1862. Vol. IV was *Quatre lettres sur la Mexique,* 1868.

Brown, John (vicar of Newcastle-upon-Tyne), *A dissertation on the rise, union and power, the progressions, separations and corruptions of poetry and music,* London 1763.

Catlin, George, *Letters and notes on the manners, customs and condition of the North American Indians. Written during eight years' travel amongst the wildest tribes of Indians in North America, in 1832, 33, 34, 35, 36, 37, 38 and 39,* New York 1841; Philadelphia 1857; London 1880; Philadelphia 1913; Edinburgh 1926 (with varying numbers of illustrations by the author).

Clavigero, Francisco J., *Historia antigua de México,* 2 vols., México 1944; 4 vols., México 1945.

Cogolludo, see López.

Domenech, Emanuel, *Seven years' residence in the great deserts of North America,* 2 vols., London 1860.

Dunn, John, *History of the Oregon Territory and British North-American fur trade; with an account of the habits and customs of the principal native tribes on the northern continent,* London 1844.

Eells, Myron, 'Indian Music', *American Antiquary,* vol. I, no. 4 (1879), pp. 249-253.

Franklin, John, *Narrative of a Journey to the shores of the Polar Sea in the years 1819, 20, 21 and 22,* London, 1823; reprint, Charles E. Tuttle Company, Rutland, Vermont and Tokyo, Japan, 1970.

Garcilasso, see Vega.

Hauptmann, Moritz, ed. O. Paul, *Die Lehre von der Harmonik,* Leipzig 1868.

Heriot, George, *Travels through the Canadas; to which is subjoined a comparative View of the Manners and Customs of several of the Indian nations of North and South America,* London 1807; Philadelphia 1813.

Herrera Tordesillas, Antonio de, *Historia general de los hechos de los castellanos en las islas y tierra firme del Mar Océano,* Madrid 1601-15; Madrid 1726-27; 17 vols., Madrid 1934-1957.

Ixtlilxóchitl, Fernando de Alva, *Obras históricas,* 2 vols., México 1952.

Jones, Sir William, *On the Musical Modes of the Hindus,* in William Jones and N. Augustus Willard, *Music of India,* Calcutta (Susil Gupta India Private) 1962.

Keating, William H., *Narrative of an expedition to the source of St. Peter's river, lake Winnepeek, lake of the Woods, etc., etc., performed in the year 1823,* Philadelphia 1824.

López Cogolludo, Diego, *Historia de Yucathan,* Madrid 1688; Merida 1867-68.

Loskiel, Georg H., *Geschichte der Mission der evangelischen Brüder unter den Indianen in Nordamerika,* Barby 1789; English trans. by Christian I. La Trobe, London 1794.

Mallery, Garrick, *A collection of gesture-signs and signals of the North American Indians,* Washington 1880.

McKnight, Charles, *Our western border one hundred years ago,* Philadelphia 1875; Chicago 1902.

Nebel, Carl, *Voyage pittoresque et archéologique dans la partie la plus intéressante du Mexique,* Paris 1836.

Oviedo y Valdés, Gonzalo Fernández de (1478-1557), *Historia general y natural de las Indias,* 3 pts. in 4 vols., Madrid 1851-55; ed. Juan Pérez de Tudela Bueso, 5 vols., Madrid 1959.

Paul, Oskar, *Die absolute Harmonik der Griechen,* Leipzig, 1866.

Powell, John Wesley, *Down the Colorado; diary of the first trip through the Grand Canyon,* 1869; abridged ed., New York 1969 (and other eds.).

Powers, Stephen, *Tribes of California* (Contributions to North American Ethnology, vol. III), Washington 1877.

Rafinesque-Smaltz, Constantine S., *The American Nations*, Philadelphia 1836.

Riggs, Thomas L., *Grammar and Dictionary of the Dakota Language* (Smithsonian Contributions to Knowledge, Washington 1848, etc., vol. IV).

Sahagún, Bernardino de, *Florentine Codex; General History of the Things of New Spain*, Bks. 1-5, 7-12, trans. Arthur J.O. Anderson and Charles E. Dibble, 4 vols., Santa Fe 1950-1963.

Schoolcraft, Henry R., *Archives of aboriginal knowledge . . . original papers laid before Congress*, 6 vols., Philadelphia 1860.

Stephens, John L., *Incidents of travel in Yucatan*, 2 vols., London and New York 1843.

Tagore, Rabindranath, *English Verses set to Hindu Music*, Calcutta 1875.

Torquemada, Juan de, *Los veintiún libros rituales y Monarchia Indiana*, Seville 1615; 3 vols., Madrid 1723; reprint of 1723 ed., México 1969.

Traill, Thomas S., 'Dissertation on a Peruvian Musical Instrument like the Syrinx of the Ancients', *Transactions of the Royal Society of Edinburgh* XX (1853), pp. 121-130.

Vega, Garcilaso de la, *Primera parte de los Comentarios Reales*, Lisbon 1609; *Histoire des Incas*, Amsterdam 1637; *Les commentaires royaux ou l'histoire des Incas*, trans. Alain Gheerbrant, Paris 1959; *Comentarios reales*, ed. Montserrat Martí Brugueras, Barcelona 1968; *Royal Commentaries of the Incas and General History of Peru*, trans. Harold V. Livermore, 2 vols., Austin 1966.

Vétromile, Eugene, *The Abnakis and their history. Or, historical notices on the aborigines of Acadia*, New York 1866.

Veytia, Mariano, *Historia antigua de Mejico*, 3 vols., México 1836.

Westphal, Rudolf, *Elemente des musikalische Rhythmus mit besondere Richtsicht auf unserer Opernmusik*, pt. I, Jena 1872.

Wilkes, Charles, *Narrative of the United States exploring expedition, during the years 1838-42*, 5 vols., Philadelphia 1845.